Bathroom Ideas You Can Use

Secrets & Solutions for Freshening Up the Hardest-Working Room in Your House

CHRIS PETERSON

**Creative Publishing
international**

MINNEAPOLIS, MINNESOTA
www.creativepub.com

Creative Publishing international

Creative Publishing international, Inc.
400 First Avenue North, Suite 400
Minneapolis, Minnesota 55401
1-800-328-0590
www.creativepub.com

Printed in China

10 9 8 7 6 5 4 3 2

Library of Congress Cataloging-in-Publication Data

Peterson, Chris, 1961-
   Bathroom ideas you can use : secrets & solutions for
freshening up the hardest-working room in your house /
by Chris Peterson.
      pages cm
   ISBN 978-1-58923-722-3 (softcover)
   1. Bathrooms--Remodeling. 2. Interior decoration.
I. Title.

TH4816.3.B37P435 2013
747.7'8--dc23

                    2012042825

Editor: Jordan Wiklund
Design Manager: Brad Springer
Page Layout: Kim Winscher

Contents

4 Introduction

10 Bathrooms by Size

    11 Powder Rooms & Half-Baths

    16 Detached & Guest Bathrooms

    24 Large & Master Baths

32 Scintillating Surfaces

    33 Tile Style

    40 Fantastic Floors

    48 Eye-Catching Vanity Counters

54 Beautiful Storage Spaces

    55 Perfect Vanities

    62 Handy Cabinets & Shelves

72 Bathing in Style

    73 Gorgeous Bathtubs

        73 Freestanding

        80 Alcove

        84 Corner

        86 Drop-In

    94 Luxury Shower Enclosures

104 Superb Fixtures

    105 Fashionable Toilets & Bidets

    110 Chic Sink Colors

    111 Chic Drop-In Sinks

    116 Chic Wall-Mount Sinks

    120 Chic Pedestal & Console Sinks

    124 Chic Vessel Sinks

130 Exceptional Hardware

    131 Divine Faucets

    136 Superior Showerheads

    140 Fantastic Tub Faucets

142 The Well-Lit Bathroom

    143 Marvelous Vanity Lights

    146 Ideal General Fixtures

150 Bathroom Extras

    151 Attractive Universal Design

    154 Handy Makeup Areas

    156 Super Saunas

    158 Stunning Skylights and Bath Windows

    164 Towel Warmers

    166 Mirror Style

    170 Exceptional Accents

174 Resources

Introduction

More than any other room in the house, a bathroom's design must effectively combine form and function. It's not always an easy balance, but get it right and you make this essential room much more comfortable, safer and a stunning part of your home's design.

Any discussion about bathroom design must actually cover three different spaces: the powder room or half-bath; the separate or guest bath; and the master bathroom. Each presents different design opportunities and challenges, but the basics of sound design underlying successful bathroom style are the same no matter what size the room may be. For instance, safety is the paramount concern in any bathroom because of the combination of water and slick surfaces. Hygiene and cleanliness are also natural issues to consider whenever you choose materials and fixtures for a bathroom design.

Whatever the particulars, one of the great things about a bathroom is that it doesn't take much to renew the look of the room. A design update can entail a quick makeover or a complete remodel. Add a new faucet, showerhead and towel bars, and you introduce fresh new flair to the room. A little paint and a

REPEAT SHAPES FOR A SOOTHING, SUBTLE EFFECT. Bathroom design details don't need to be ostentatious or over the top to make a big impact. This simple black-and-white bathroom is made more stylish with the addition of a frosted-glass divider at the foot of the tub, a simple black bathmat over an understated sisal rug and unusual shelves that offer dynamic shapes and plenty of visual interest. All the fixtures are kept simple and white, and contemporary faucet fittings reinforce the room's uncomplicated—yet beautiful—aesthetic.

refinished vanity can do the same. Of course, you can change the look even more dramatically if you're willing to resurface the walls or floors, or make bigger changes such as adding a standalone shower enclosure, a bidet or a jetted tub. Larger changes can also make the room more usable. Add his-and-her sinks, and you alleviate marital friction and make the morning bathroom rush hour a lot less stressful for everyone.

Luxury, though, is the highest calling for a bathroom design. Steam fittings in a shower stall, towel warmers, super-deep soaking tubs and mini-saunas are all ways to turn the bathroom into less of a purely functional space and more of a spa-like experience. The examples that follow illustrate the full range of possibilities for your bathroom. Choose the options that suit your space, your life, your budget and your tastes, and turn this functional space into a more comfortable design gem that adds to the look, comfort and enjoyment of your home.

LUXURIATE YOUR BATHROOM WITH PERIOD-STYLE CHAIRS AND ENDTABLES. Turn to unexpected style features such as the chandelier and period-style chair used in this room and include top-of-the-line fixtures such as this drop-in whirlpool tub. Captured in a highly detailed custom oval surround, this model includes heated backrests, 36 jets, molded armrests, color-matched grab bars and room enough for two. A luxury shower stall or bathtub like this not only elevates the bathroom's look, it can vastly improve your day-to-day life.

Introduction

USE DIFFERENT PATTERNS AND TEXTURES ON BATHROOM BUMPOUTS. Institute high style in your bathroom by including a mix of textures and patterns to provide increased visual interest anywhere the eye settles. The sleek white marble floor in this lavish bathroom competes for attention with the showy silver-patterned wallpaper framing the bumpout. The simple modern fixtures and vanity, as well as a glass shower enclosure, reinforce the luxurious style driving the room's aesthetic. Notice that as stylish as the space is, function and storage have not been sacrificed to the design.

OUTFIT A BATHROOM WITH A WALK-IN CLOSET. The southwestern flair of this en suite bathroom and walk-in closet combo features a vanity and storage that not only match the cabinetry in the closet and dressing area but also look custom-made for the space. There is a vanity and matching storage furniture to suit any bathroom—even if the room has adobe walls and irregular stone pavers for a floor.

UNEXPECTED FURNISHINGS INVIGORATE BATHROOMS, LIKE THIS EXTERIOR TUB SPOUT AND CHAISE LOUNGE. Add unexpected elements to a bathroom—especially a large bathroom such as this—to pump up the visual interest. The chaise lounge reinforces the notion of the room as a spa retreat. The open shelving with rolled-up towels is a great way to store attractive textiles, but it also provides rounded shapes that contrast the overwhelmingly linear design of the room, up to and including the stylish spout outside the tub. Shape and line are as much a part of the well-designed bathroom as color and texture.

SINK FIXTURES INCORPORATED INTO A MIRROR OR WALL ARE NOVEL DESIGN DECISIONS. Mounting sink fixtures through the mirror is an innovative and chic choice for bathrooms. The temperature controls are left on the vanity, while waterproof backsplash tiles create a clear border from countertop to wall. The matte black tile has a scintillating surface relief that invites the hand as well as the eye. Small details such as this can dial your bathroom design up a notch with a modest investment, regardless of the size of the room.

Introduction

MATCH THE TOILET TO THE ROOM STYLE. Reinforce your bathroom's design theme with your choice of toilets. The available selection of toilet styles is greater than ever before and, as shown here, includes some eye-catching shapes. This bathroom is equipped with both toilet and bidet, and as is done in almost every case, the two are a matched set. These modern-style fixtures are also low-flow, which is not only the socially responsible way to go, it's also mandated by many local, regional and state ordinances.

WALL SCONCES EMIT SOFT AND SOOTHING LIGHT THAT IS PERFECT FOR BATHROOMS. Choose lighting fixtures to not only serve the function, but also add a flashy form to the bathroom's design. Sconces, like this matched pair, are perfect for bringing a bit of drama into the room. Notice how the blown-glass shades on these units work perfectly with the wall paint color and also complement the handsome vanity-and-mirror combination. If you have your heart set on colorful light fixtures, it's a wise idea to bring paint and vanity finish samples with you when you go shopping.

CUSTOM TILE MAKES A SHOWER STUNNING. Looking to impress in your bathroom? If you're willing to spend a bit more, you can't go wrong with a custom-tiled shower enclosure like the one shown here. Distinctive motif indicators like the arch used in this shower opening, the alcove shelf and the wall detailing add even more flair. The mix of tile shapes, colors and sizes is a sure way to keep the eye moving and interested. A bench makes this particular shower as luxurious to use as it is to look at.

UPGRADE YOUR SHOWER TO TRANSFORM YOUR LIFE. Create an unforgettable morning ritual by including multiple showerheads in your shower. The body sprayers shown here combine with an overhead rainwater showerhead to turn a simple shower into a hedonistic daily indulgence. A rail-mounted, handheld showerhead increases the adaptability of this shower and makes it even more luxurious. Low-flow versions (pictured here) let you enjoy the sumptuous experience knowing it's eco-friendly as well.

Bathrooms by Size

One of the key differences among bathrooms is their size. The smallest are half-baths or powder rooms, used mostly by guests. Detached, or guest, bathrooms usually serve more than one bedroom and often have a bathtub shower rather than a separate shower and tub. Master bathrooms are grander spaces that usually include one or more luxury features such as a two-person whirlpool tub or a large, standalone shower enclosure.

Bathrooms of different sizes call for different design approaches. Half-baths are generally high-traffic areas where conserving space is a big concern and storage less so. However, because people spend less time in a powder room or half-bath, and because smaller surface areas and fixtures translate to less expense overall, you can often go a bit wilder in designing a powder room than you would a larger bathroom. These bathrooms are often vividly colored and include distinctive sinks, faucets or lighting.

Detached baths usually need to serve more than one person, often including both guests and family members. Comfort is king in the detached bath, and small luxuries bring a big bang to the room. If you can carve out space for a separate shower enclosure or large soaking tub, you add immeasurably to the luxury and perceived sophistication of the room. Special tile, standout sinks and chic storage solutions all go a long way toward creating a distinctive detached bath design.

Master baths—whether they are actually connected to a master bedroom or not—are opportunities to bring hardcore luxury into your day-to-day world. Install steam fittings in a shower, a two-person whirlpool bath, or his-and-her sinks and you make the room more inviting to look at, easier to use, and a wonderful place to unwind after the pressures of a long day.

ADORN POWDER ROOMS WITH SMALL FIXTURES TO INCREASE THE VISUAL SPACE. As this photo clearly shows, you'll find fixtures, furnishings and fittings full of flair for even the most modest powder room space. The cylindrical vanity features a small amount of concealed storage, just right for the few essentials necessary in a tiny bathroom. Chic pendant lights hanging on each side of the understated mirror spice up the look of the room and illuminate what can often be a fairly shadowy space.

WOOD IS GOOD IN SMALL BATHROOMS. With its horizontal wood paneling, this room boasts an eclectic, slightly country feel. The informal look is kept from being kitschy by the classic, solid styling of the pedestal sink and elongated, one-piece toilet. Those fixtures are restrained anchor points in a room design that includes a funky round mirror and casual wicker basket towel storage. It's a lot of style for a small space.

SPLURGE ON MATERIALS FOR POWDER ROOMS. The gray tile covering the floor and walls in this bathroom establishes a very sophisticated look, one made richer with a sleek wall-mounted sink and vanity and wall-mounted toilet. The wall-mount faucet reinforces the modern vibe, as do the elegant hanging pendants. The room includes a cool, water-conserving flush actuator on the wall, providing dual-flush capability.

PEDESTAL SINKS HIDE THE PLUMBING IN SMALL BATHROOMS. Now that you've hidden the plumbing, why not show off the room? Bright white wainscoting looks fantastic for country, informal or contemporary bathrooms. If you don't feel up to working with wood, you can buy simple polyurethane wainscoting kits that make installing a surface like this easy—especially in a room where the wall surface is limited. The lack of clutter allows the well-styled pedestal sink and wainscoting to shine.

SAVE SPACE BY GOING VERTICAL. Make a powder room seem more spacious with wall-hung fixtures and storage. The toilet and vanity counter used here leave plenty of space underneath, which gives the visual impression of larger floor space. Wall-mounts are a clean, sleek choice, appropriate for modern or contemporary bathrooms; they look a bit out of place in a more traditional or period bathroom. Mounting fixtures on the wall in a bathroom creates a more polished look by concealing the plumbing that services the fixtures.

Powder Rooms & Half-Baths

USE MULTIPLE MIRRORS TO OPEN UP THE ROOM. You can often get the most out of a small powder room by approaching the design more like you would a main room, rather than another bathroom. This tiny bathroom is a perfect example, featuring an enchanting small vanity that resembles a round console table and a round mirror that might otherwise be found in an entryway. The mirror is supplemented with an adjacent gilt-framed mirror, which opens up the room. A small chandelier provides just the right amount of light as it might otherwise do in a foyer, dining room or hallway. The features combine to give this powder room an appeal beyond that basic bathroom style.

Bathrooms by Size   13

Powder Rooms & Half-Baths

SHOW OFF HALF BATHROOMS AND POWDER ROOMS WITH FINE FLOOR TREATMENTS. More expensive flooring might not be practical in a larger, busier bathroom, but it's perfect here. This colonial-style half-bath features lovely wood wainscoting and detailed casework, as well as a stunning oak floor. The light honey color of the floor and the unusual height of the wainscoting serve to raise the ceiling and increase the sense of space in the bathroom.

MATCH WALL EFFECTS TO FIXTURES FOR SUBTLE BEAUTY. Sponging, rag-rolling, stippling and other effects are perfect for such a small, contained space, and they create visual excitement without overwhelming the room. Choose colors carefully to avoid jarring contrasts between the base and top coats and complement the fixtures and furniture in the room—as the brown paint on these walls complements the formal vanity and serves as the perfect backdrop for an ornate mirror frame.

USE TILE, RECESSED WINDOWS, MIRRORS AND BASE MOLDING IN TANDEM TO ENHANCE A SMALL SPACE. Contrary to conventional wisdom, multiple fixtures in the right dark colors can enhance a small space and actually make it seem larger. The colors in this two-tone paint scheme are separated by a band of tiles, a technique that works wonderfully no matter what size the room or what colors you use. Neutral colors tone down a busy aesthetic.

KEEP THE SMALLEST SPACES SIMPLE. If your toilet and sink are positioned next to each other in a corner, use a small sink to avoid crowding someone sitting on the toilet. Always choose fixtures and position them with the space between kept firmly in mind. Notice that no storage or other furniture has been placed in the corner; leaving the space relatively free ensures easy movement between toilet and sink and creates more visual space as well. The choice of white walls and floor, with a basic decorative border of patterned tiles, visually opens up the room.

Detached & Guest Baths

LOW KEY WORKS IN GUEST BATHS. Sometimes a subdued design provides the most welcoming comfort in a space used by many people, so don't hesitate to go low key in your guest bath. Here, a gold bathmat, towels and other accents liven up the room's classic gray-and-white scheme. An oak hardwood floor provides an unexpected look underfoot, and crisp chrome accents and fixtures in the bath and shower provide an upscale polish.

TRADE A BATH FOR A SHOWER. Turn a simple detached bath into a grander space by exchanging a standard bathtub for a fully tiled shower enclosure. If you're going to go to the trouble of creating a large walk-in enclosure such as this, tiling it on all surfaces will make it that much more special. A tile color that stands out from the other colors in the room is one way to draw attention to this very special feature.

NEO-ANGLES SAVE SPACE. Add a shower to a bathroom that seems squeezed for space by using a neo-angle shower kit. These types of shower enclosures tuck into a corner and take up very little floor space, making them appropriate for even modestly sized guest baths. The unit here was built with a metal frame, but you can also find more modern-looking frameless neo-angle enclosures. You can build a neo-angle shower from scratch or turn to one of the many kits available that make the process easier and quicker—not to mention increasing your style choices.

DESIGN TO THE ROOM'S AVAILABLE SPACE AND SHAPE. Design a detached bathroom to optimize the space, getting as much as you can from the room. This long, narrow guest bathroom features a slim—but deep—soaking tub that offers a lot of luxury in a small footprint. Likewise, the glass walls of the shower enclosure are not only chic and afford maximum light penetration, they are also much thinner than a traditional wall, taking up far less space (both visually and physically). A narrow solid-surface vanity top with integral his-and-her sinks caps off a space-efficient and understated yet powerful bathroom design.

CHOOSE FIXTURES TO SUIT AVAILABLE SPACE. Outfit an attic guest bath with space considerations in mind. This compact room features a tiny cabinet where the vanity would have gone, because there was no plumbing for a sink. The shower enclosure is positioned for maximum headroom, and the cabinet supplies just enough storage for the essentials (such as a back-up supply of toilet paper). Often, in guest bathrooms, you have to make the most of the space the architecture gives you.

USE ROUND SHAPES FOR INFORMAL, YET EFFECTIVE, DESIGN. This is especially true in detached bathrooms, which tend to feature low-key designs that verge on boring. This room includes a repetitive oval shape in the mirror, sink and toilet tank—shapes that buffer the wealth of lines and sharp angles in the room. Introducing round or oval shapes makes a room design seem less stiff and less formal and can—as this room clearly shows—make a bathroom appear more inviting.

Detached & Guest Baths

SAVE SPACE WITH A BUILT-IN CORNER TUB. Detached bathrooms can be squeezed for space, but that doesn't mean you have to downgrade the luxury. You can include a jetted tub with a useful built-in surround by tucking the structure into a corner. You can also install a standard apron tub with plain sides for even more space savings. In either case, the placement leaves the floor area clear and gives the room a more spacious feel.

TUB SURROUNDS ARE GREAT SOLUTIONS FOR GUEST BATHROOMS. Turn to a three-piece tub surround for an easy, handsome surface treatment in a guest bathroom's bathtub shower. These solid panels are inexpensive and available in a wide range of colors and styles, from the very plain to the more ornate, such as the faux tile and ledges shown here. They are usually formed of fiberglass, polymers or other synthetic materials, which means they are lightweight, waterproof, easy to install and fairly durable. Choose versions with integral shelves, cubbies or other features depending on how many people use the tub and shower.

SIMPLE COLOR SCHEMES ARE INVITING. You will find elegance in simplicity when you work with what you have in your guest bathroom. Here, the room's casework is painted a clean, sharp white that emphasizes the detail without calling too much attention to it. A wall of white tile behind the tub is an uncomplicated treatment that is still quite handsome, and the simple blue-and-bright white color scheme is ideal in a space where cleanliness comes first. This bathroom is proof that you don't need expensive design bells and whistles to create a truly lovely space.

Detached & Guest Baths

EMPHASIZE SPACE AND SUBTLETY WITH MINIMAL FURNISHINGS AND ACCENTS. There's no harm in keeping your bathroom design low key, especially in a smaller detached bath. Here, demure taupe ceramic tile ties together the tub and shower areas, without closing in the space as bolder, darker or more dynamic tiles might have done. The chunky wood console base for the sink provides a modest amount of style and texture, but its open construction also helps the room appear more spacious. All in all, the combination of neutral colors and simple textures and lines makes this a handsome, if understated, bathroom.

EMPHASIZE OPENNESS WITH LIGHT, FORM, AND FREE-STANDING FURNISHINGS. Bring a guest bathroom to stunning life with a minimal, modern treatment. This room features an open floor plan as striking as it is unusual. A graceful freestanding tub with a sweeping form tops an eye-catching marble floor. The modern tigerwood vanity boasts an off-center sink with a sleek modern faucet. Although this is an extreme design style, in the right house, it would be a showstopper.

Detached &
Guest Baths

BLEND STORAGE WHEN SPACE IS TIGHT. Make the most of available space for a busy family bathroom with careful cabinetry selections. Ample storage has been introduced into this small bathroom with just the right mix of top and bottom cabinets, along with a corner unit. The cabinets were bought as a set, which is why they blend so well together. But they have the same detailing you'd find in custom cabinetry, including fine drawer molding and glass-front doors.

SMALL LIGHTS AND LARGE MIRRORS ARE PERFECT PARTNERS. Pick style elements according to how well they will work in the limited space of a guest bathroom. This well-appointed room includes a deep, narrow soaking tub that fits neatly under the room's window without hogging floor space. Small but incredibly tasteful light fixtures leave plenty of room for wide mirrors while supplying drop-dead good looks and plenty of illumination. The detailing on front of the vanity and the sophisticated color combinations are high-style indicators that take up no space at all.

ACCENTUATE ALCOVES WITH TILE. Some vanities are too large to comfortably fit inside a guest or family bathroom but work well in the confined space of an alcove. By tiling around it, the cramped space is transformed into an eye-catching focal point. Here, the wood used for the adjacent storage cabinets matches the trim on the bath deck, and the combination of shelving and drawer space ensures that there is a place for everything that needs to be stored in this shared bathroom.

RESTRAIN FOR ELEGANCE. Exercise restraint in designing a large, opulent bathroom and create a stunningly elegant space by focusing the attention on the few key features that most deserve it. The design of this bathroom is monochromatic, but the lack of bright or vivid color allows distinctive border tiles to jump out. The understated design also gives prominence to a lovely bow window and the view it frames. When it comes to bathroom design, you don't necessarily need to shout to get attention.

REPETITIVE TEXTURES UNIFY DESIGN. Outfit a large luxurious bathroom with a suite of matching cabinets to create a unified design and a fluid visual flow. The stylish raised-panel cabinets here even match the bathtub apron, and the abundant storage they offer ensures that clutter will never be a problem. When choosing a suite of cabinets, consider bonus features such as the dressing desk shown here—extras that make the bathroom even more special.

IDENTIFIABLE DESIGNS WORK WELL IN LARGE BATHROOMS. A recognizable design like the Asian-inspired look in this room is perfect for a larger, luxury bathroom. The stepped platform with a drop-in tub is a particularly effective use of the abundant space, giving the room a high-end bathhouse feel. Insightful use of a traditional-styled toilet and fixtures with simple lines complements the rest of the design and lets the standout elements, such as the textured wall coverings, grab the lion's share of attention.

DIVIDE LARGE ROOMS INTO FUNCTIONAL AREAS. Where your bathroom is large enough, consider dividing it into separate functional areas. A divider wall in this room separates the bathing area from the sink and vanity. A large cabinet unit positioned in an alcove provides enough storage for clothes, making the sink area also a dressing area—another function that can be added to a large bathroom.

CONSISTENT COLOR SCHEMES ARE MORE CRUCIAL IN LARGE BATHROOMS. Keep your bathroom color scheme under control to maintain a calming, serene feel to the room. Color schemes are especially important in larger bathrooms, where the color interactions play out more dramatically. The neutral scheme used in this master bath certainly creates a soothing feel, but the room hardly lacks for visual excitement. A wide range of neutral tones— from beige to almost black—and a dynamic mix of tile sizes, shapes and configurations combine with stunning decorative elements to make a bathroom design that invites the visitor to linger.

RELY ON WINDOWS TO LIGHT LARGE BATHROOMS. This light-soaked bathroom enjoys a wealth of open floor space; a wicker chaise longue creates an area for pure relaxation—a common designation for large, luxurious bathrooms. Add furniture to your spacious bathroom to add function. Notice that this room doesn't scrimp on style elsewhere either; pebbled tile covers the bath deck and shower surround, matching the yellow monochromatic color scheme.

RESTRAIN FURNISHINGS IF DETAILS ARE YOUR FOCUS. Don't be afraid to let one or two signature features dominate the design of your master bathroom. This bathroom is an example of how an otherwise sedate and restrained design can showcase a distinctive decorative element. The neutral color scheme and lack of detailing create a calm atmosphere, one that serves as a backdrop to an incredible stone wall surface behind the vanity and a pile of river rocks used as sculpture.

LESS CAN BE MORE, MUCH MORE. You don't necessarily need to fill a large bathroom with storage or other features; let the space speak for itself to create a stunningly minimal look. Here, the impressive half-wall frames the mirror and vanity, offsetting the freestanding bathtub. The ebonized wood floor sets the stage for a very Spartan room style that includes an interesting freestanding tub with integral ledge, a modern off-center vanity, and a wonderful rug that is a treat for the feet as well as the eyes. Slatted wood screens help define the space, but mostly, it is a room left open and impressive.

OPULENCE MAKES SMALL SEEM BIG. Just because your master bathroom is not especially large is no reason for it to lack luxury. As this room shows, even a small bathroom can appear and function as a sumptuous space. The rich look is created by using a wealth of dark-wood details, a tiled wall surface, and specific accents that bring a huge dose of style, including a small chandelier and a large mirror propped up next to the bath. The mirror not only provides a lovely decorative element, it also serves to visually expand the room.

USE ACCENT LIGHTING FOR UNIQUE SAFETY AND COMFORT. Turn to the uncommon for an even more special master bath design. Recessed halogen lights make the tile sparkle, but more importantly, they provide added safety for anyone getting out of the tub after enjoying a relaxing candlelit bath. Spotlights in the base of the tub platform are also unusual elements. Accent lighting in the bathroom inevitably serves two purposes—decoration and safety. What's more, the marble tiles that cover the surfaces in this luxury bath are a predictable choice. The use of three long shelves in place of a traditional vanity is not.

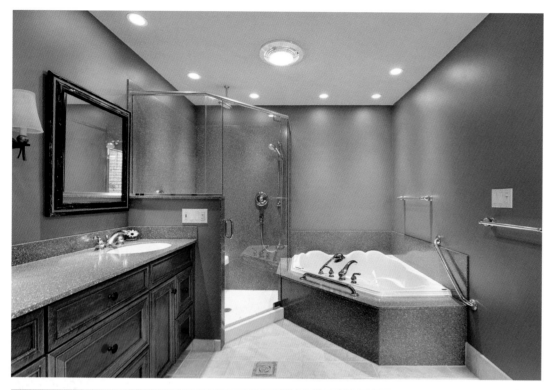

USE ANGLES TO MAXIMIZE SPACE. Play the angles to get the most out of a narrow master bathroom. The shower and tub in this room are a perfect example of how to fit luxury in a skinny space. Angled back against one another, the features make for an interesting mix of lines, but they supply full-scale bathing in an abbreviated space. Getting the most out of any bathroom is, to one degree or another, always about positioning major features in the room in a space-efficient way.

USE A WATER CLOSET TO MAXIMIZE EFFICIENCY IN BUSY BATHROOMS. These small, self-contained rooms-within-a-room essentially ensure that more than one person can use the bathroom at a time, and they hide away the least attractive fixture in any bathroom. Water closets themselves can be made luxurious with the addition of a wired-in sound system, magazine racks, special heaters, or even a phone or intercom connection.

USE CROWN MOLDING OR OTHER ACCENTS TO TIE ROOMS TOGETHER. Be design-wise and integrate elements in your master bathroom that tie the room to the bedroom or any other spaces connected directly to the bathroom. One of the most effective ways to do this is to use the same crown molding throughout the rooms as was done here, with the distinctive wood molding that matches the custom-made vanity. You can also unify adjoining rooms with wall color, window treatments or even similarly shaped or colored accents. The more design elements contiguous rooms share, the more pleasing the aesthetic is to behold.

Scintillating Surfaces

Surface coverings are often the most visually powerful part of a bathroom's design. Your bathroom's floor, walls and vanity counter all offer incredible opportunities to create stunning focal points. That's the good news. The better news is that there has never been a greater selection of surfacing materials from which to choose.

Aside from being beautiful, the only limitation on potential claddings for your bathroom surfaces is that they be waterproof or at least resistant to moisture, comfortable to the touch and cleanable. That leaves a lot of home center aisles to explore.

Where once tile was ubiquitous, many new options have emerged, including laminate floorings that replicate the look of materials from stone to tile, eco-friendly Marmoleum click flooring, specially sealed wood wall panels and polyurethane moldings and wainscoting, to name just a few.

Of course, tile remains a favorite, not least because there are more types than you can count. Choose from glass, finished or unfinished stone, ceramic or porcelain or metal, and your decisions have just begun. Any color under the rainbow is available in tile, and potential shapes and sizes are nearly limitless. You can even pick from textures ranging from rough and matte to completely smooth and shiny.

One thing is for certain, though; whether you're leaning toward traditional ceramic tile or drawn to more exotic seagrass wall coverings and bamboo flooring, surface coverings in the bathroom have an outsized impact. They can set the entire style for the room and often dominate the color palette. And because bathroom surface areas are some of the smallest of any room, you can usually incorporate a pricey, sumptuous, one-of-a-kind surface without killing your budget.

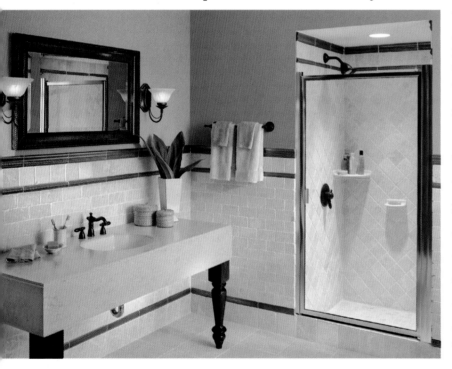

DIFFERENT STONE TEXTURES WORK WELL TOGETHER. Visual interest is multiplied on these surfaces by varying tile size and shape throughout. As beautiful as real stone surfaces such as these may be, be sure that any porous stone is sealed against water penetration. You can use any of a number of sealant products that will most likely need to be regularly reapplied, or you can purchase presealed stone tiles that need no further maintenance.

FEW SURFACES BLEND COLOR AS WELL AS TILE. As a general rule, use large-format tiles in large bathrooms and small-format tiles in smaller spaces. Of course, as this bathroom illustrates, design rules are meant to be broken. By isolating smaller mosaic tiles to specific areas—and using solid surface coverings for the greater surface area—the designer of this room has added huge visual interest and color to a clean, contemporary space. You can use vibrant mosaic tiles to define a specific area, even in a larger space, as long as sufficient "negative" space in the form of an unbroken surface can relieve the busy look of the smaller tile.

Walls of Wow

MIX TILE AND GLASS FOR DRAMATIC SURFACE TREATMENTS. Consider metal tiles to make your bathroom walls the stars of the room. Metal-tiled surfaces offer unusual appearances that sometimes fool the eye but always intrigue the viewer. The tiles are as easy to clean as glass or ceramic tiles are and amplify light in useful and sometimes extraordinary ways (like the reflection in the countertop in this picture). Exploit the allure of a metal surface by using a single color tile, or mix and match with other sizes or finishes—or even intermingle metal with glass or ceramic tiles. The design possibilities are endless.

CONNECT A FLOOR TREATMENT TO A WALL WITH TILE. Intermingle tiled wall surfaces for stunning contrasts and complements. A row of green mosaic tiles has been run across the backsplash in this bathroom and further into a section of the shower wall that is tiled floor to ceiling with white subway tile. The classic shape and bright white color of the shower-wall tile helps make the small band of mosaic tile pop, and the interaction draws favorable attention to both surfaces.

USE TILE TO FRAME AND HIGHLIGHT FEATURES. Define the different areas of a bathroom with different tile treatments to give the eye easy cues to follow. In this Tuscan-style tiled bath, a vertical grid of brown tiles outlines the sitting area, while a chair-rail border of tiles separates sink from mirror and visually sets the sink area apart. Top and bottom borders of darker tile unify the areas where water is used. It's a fascinating look that makes visual sense.

USE INSET TILES TO COMPLETE A GRAND SCHEME. You can choose tile to create a very specific style in your bathroom. This room has been tiled for a formal, period-style look. Special, highly detailed border tiles called "listellos" capture plainer white and beige field tiles, with insets marking both the wall and bathtub. Gold accents in the form of a gilt mirror frame and faucets are the icing on the cake of a regal bathroom design that would be right at home in a palace.

COMPLEMENT LARGE TILES WITH SIMPLE FURNISHINGS. Take a cue from designers and use large tiles in larger bathrooms. Not only do they look more appropriate in a spacious room, large tiles take less time and effort to install. If you're using a sizeable field of large tiles—like the wall behind this bathtub—consider color very carefully. Play it safe by using tiles with a minimal amount of color variation tile to tile.

EXPLOIT TILE COLOR POSSIBILITIES. Create incredibly stunning bathroom walls by using tile in unique elegant colors, such as the luminescent green here, and combining the color with a patterned surface, such as the undulations on part of this vanity wall. The pattern leads the eye from side to side and breaks up what is a fairly restrained modern design. The undulating tile surface also produces highlights that change depending on where you are in the room and how the bathroom is lit. This sort of changeable design element creates an interactive and sophisticated bathroom.

FRAME A MIRROR IN TILE. Make a plain vanity mirror fancier—especially in a room with detailed tile work, such as this bathroom—by creating a frame with tile. The rounded-profile tile is ideal and looks just like a custom-made frame. You can use tiles to create mirror frames from subtle to funky, and because the exposure is so minimal, the frame tile does not necessarily need to match any tile you've used on the floor or walls. It's your chance to be a bit creative with your tile selection.

SAMPLE TILE DESIGN BEFORE BUYING. When you're shopping for a very special and unique border treatment for your bathroom walls, actually lay out the tiles so that you get a true sense of how they work together. Designs on paper won't give you an accurate idea of how different tile textures, shapes and colors will combine. Laying the tiles out is also an easy way to quickly edit any design you've picked, interchanging the layout with tiles that are on hand.

Tile Style

PORCELAIN OFFERS MAXIMUM VARIETY. Porcelain tile is your go-to option for a hard, waterproof surface in a nearly unlimited range of colors, shapes and sizes. Tile manufacturers also produce versions with imprint textures, which provide a relief surface that is not only visually interesting but also slip resistant. The color of the tile goes all the way through and can't be scratched off. Some types of porcelain tile look like cut stone.

METAL IS UNUSUAL, BUT DISTINCTIVE. Willing to plunk down a bit more for your tiles? If so, you can consider a wall of stainless steel or other metal tiles. These offer one-of-a-kind appearances and are virtually indestructible. The tiles come in finishes from high-gloss polished, unpolished and several in between, as well as many different colors. Metal tiles are offered in all the standard shapes and sizes, which is why they are often used to accent ceramic-, stone- or porcelain-tiled surfaces.

CERAMIC SAVES MONEY. Turn to ceramic tiles for a relatively inexpensive option with about the same design diversity as porcelain tiles. You'll find ceramic tiles that convincingly mimic stone surfaces for a fraction of the price. Textured varieties are used where slip resistance is needed. Ceramic tiles are also incredibly durable and can last decades in a bathroom (although the grout between tiles inevitably requires maintenance, cleaning and sealing).

GLASS GIVES GUSTO. Pick glass tile where you want luminous colors. Glass bathroom tiles are usually backed with white latex so that the colors are fairly bright even when the tone itself is more subdued. Glass tile reflects light, making this a great option for smaller bathrooms or those that don't receive natural light. Colored glass tile is colored through and through, although gloss surfaces will show scratches—consequently, glass tile is usually not used in rough-and-tumble family baths that see a lot of traffic or use by children.

STONE IS LAVISH. Natural stone tiles offer you an incredible variety of looks and surface textures—some of the most luxurious and sophisticated in bathroom design. The price range for these tiles is equally as varied. Polished and sealed stone is preferable so that the stone doesn't absorb water and undermine the adhesive used to secure the tiles. Tiles with irregular surfaces are often best underfoot to prevent slips and falls. Stone tiles are excellent complements to other tiles when used over the span of a tiled surface or as a decorative border row.

MOSAIC HAS MANY FACES. Mosaic tiles remain a favorite of homeowners everywhere. Available in most materials, the tiles are small (generally no larger than 1 x 1") and usually grouped on a mesh backing to allow for easier installation. Some mosaic tiles are crafted of individual tiles in figural or abstract designs and can be used to create a repetitive pattern or as a showcase insert in an otherwise solid-colored field of tiles. You can also find mosaics in unusual shapes, such as the hexagonal tiles shown here.

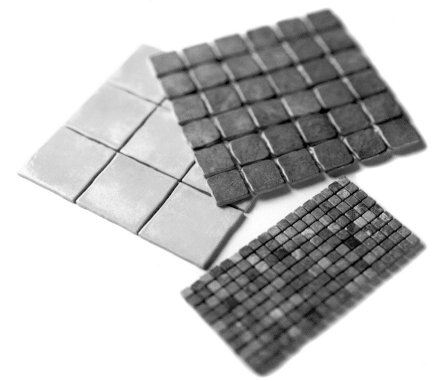

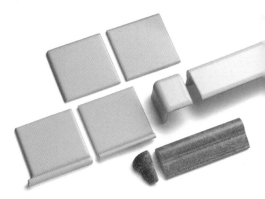

CEMENT IS FOR CUSTOMIZATION. Incorporate the unusual in your bathroom by using cement tiles. Cement tiles can be manufactured in just about any shape, size or configuration imaginable. The material can also be dyed a fantastic range of colors, and the surface can be stamped or impressed to create a regular or irregular surface pattern. Cement tiles are usually polished or otherwise sealed because water infiltration can compromise the structure of the tile.

TRIM YOUR TILES. Finish your tiled surfaces with trim tiles, specialty tiles designed to conceal the edges of field tile along the top or sides of a wall or vanity surface. These include bullnose tile, which is used to finish the edges of wall tiles that don't cover the complete wall surface, corner tiles to give a polished look at the corner of installations and many other specific tiles, such as chair or picture rail tiles. Some, such as border edge tile, can be pressed into service for interesting applications such as framing a mirror or window.

Fantastic Floors

COLOR DYNAMICALLY WITH CERAMIC. Create your own Op-Art floor with the help of ceramic tile. The cobalt blue tiles here perfectly complement the yellow-gold of the maple cabinetry, making for a captivating contemporary look. The tile has been also used to frame the top of the tub, and the vessel sinks were selected in a matching color. Choose vividly colored ceramic tiles for a sharp, stylish look in a bathroom of any size.

HARDWOOD IS UNIQUE. Turn to a hardwood floor for a distinctive, unexpected look in the bathroom. This pecan floor is specially finished to resist moisture infiltration and damage from sun exposure. The wide planks make for an informal look, and the dark brown stain adds drama. The warm feel of a wood floor underfoot is a luxury in any room, but especially a bathroom. Wood floors and alternatives such as bamboo are increasingly being offered with special finishes for use in the bathroom.

MIX TILE SIZE, COLOR AND SHAPE TO ACCENTUATE YOUR FLOORS AND WALLS. The porcelain tiles used throughout this lovely bathroom share similar finishes but exhibit an incredible amount of variety in their different shapes, sizes and colors. The border design on the floor is a classic bathroom style, and it's offset by witty faux wainscoting created with the help of long narrow tiles. The strips on the tub-surround tile tie that surface to the black border on the floor, helping unify all the surfaces in the space.

Fantastic Floors

BORDERS BUFFER BATHROOMS. If you're willing to go a little wild with tile, you can create a fun, funky, boldly colorful look that is all your own. This bathroom includes no less than seven different sizes and shapes of tile, and they have been combined in a high-energy pattern that is toned down somewhat through the use of cool blue colors throughout. This is dynamic visual interest in action; if you undertake a complex mix of tile patterns like this, start by working them out on paper.

PEBBLE FLOORS STIMULATE EYES AS WELL AS FEET. Looking for something different for an informal bathroom floor? Try pebble tiles like the floor laid in this country-style bathroom. The tiles are actual cut pebbles that lie flat and are grouped on a mesh backing—each sheet is laid just like standard tiles are. The look is very unique and fun on the feet as well. You can find pebble tiles in the matte, uniform color appearance of this floor or in a range of muted colors including blues, grays and greens—even jet black.

VINYL FLOORING IS WARM, CUSHIONY AND COST-EFFECTIVE. Comfortable underfoot, vinyl flooring comes in a vast array of styles, colors and surface textures— including the style here that mimics mosaic tile. You can buy vinyl tiles for the bathroom, but the more waterproof and permanent flooring is vinyl sheet. Just be sure to air out the room thoroughly before you use it; vinyl emits volatile organic compounds (VOCs) for some time after it's installed.

Fantastic Floors

DIFFER FLOORING IN SMALL BATHROOMS TO DEFINE THE SPACE. Where you have constructed a separate shower enclosure, differentiate key spaces in the room by differing the flooring between the shower and the main part of the bathroom. Here, a concrete floor in the bathroom proper is a very cool look and an easy-to-clean surface, but the use of mosaic glass tile in the shower enclosure defines it as separate from the rest of the room and gives the shower enclosure its own character.

GO PREFAB TO SAVE ON SHOWER ENCLOSURES. A molded, prefabricated tray base is the easiest, quickest and least-expensive way to install a standalone shower enclosure. You can order prefab trays in a number of different sizes, shapes and colors, and they can easily be matched to frameless walls, such as those shown here, to make for an easy-to-install stunner of a bathroom addition.

USE SMALL TILES TO HIGHLIGHT FIXTURES. Play it safe by following the conventional rule and use small tiles in smaller bathrooms and big tiles in larger spaces. The tiles here are a subdued gray that makes the floor and wall seem like a background canvas for the interesting fixtures, which include a contemporary wall-mounted sink and vanity and boxy cube lights over the mirror. One of the great things about tile is you can use them as a lovely background to other design elements or as showcase features in and of themselves.

Fantastic Floors

MATCH WOOD FLOORS WITH OTHER NATURAL ELEMENTS. Create a welcoming, informal appearance in your bathroom with a handsome wood floor. This tough oak floor has been finished to withstand the occasional splash of water from the tub, and it looks beautiful in a space that features a stunning freestanding bathtub with chunky wood-block "feet," a leaning towel rack made from bamboo and a simple, textured wall covering. All the elements combine to make this a simple and pleasing bathroom design.

USE TILE TO CREATE SCENES. You can lay a highly detailed floor such as this in your own bathroom using prearranged borders provided by the tile manufacturer. Retailers and manufacturers offer medallions, simple borders, special insets and complete floor centerpieces like this wave design in mesh-backed, pre-fab sheets that are incredibly easy to lay. If you like the look of mosaic tiles, consider using them to their full potential in an intricate and splashy bathroom floor design.

MIX CLASSIC AND MODERN WITH CONCRETE AND WOOD. Go with polished concrete floors for an extremely durable surface that screams modern design. This sleek floor is easy to clean and waterproof and is also fairly easy to install. However, it is a little cold on the feet during chillier months, a drawback you can deal with by setting down wood slats, as has been done in the shower area of this bathroom.

SHAG RUGS ARE CLEAN, COMFORTABLE AND FUN. Make an area rug part of your flooring and accent choices, and your feet will forever thank you. A shag rug such as the one in this modest bathroom keeps water from making the floor slippery. But more importantly, it feels wonderful on the soles of your feet. Area rugs are usually a decorative element on which it's easy to splurge; they aren't very expensive, they provide small but tangible luxury in the space, and they are easy to clean and move around as needed.

USE CONCRETE IN HIGH-TECH BATHROOMS. Concrete seems like a natural choice for the bathroom, at once durable, water resistant and inexpensive. However, concrete floors are most often used for high-tech or modern bathrooms, such as the one pictured here. The sleek X-trestle vanity and cool accessories set a cutting-edge style that the concrete surface fits right into. Polished concrete is the most popular choice, because the surface is entirely waterproof and complements a wider range of design styles. Keep in mind that concrete can be tinted every color of the rainbow and stamped with designs that not only make it look more interesting and unique, but increase the slip-resistance of the surface.

Fantastic Floors

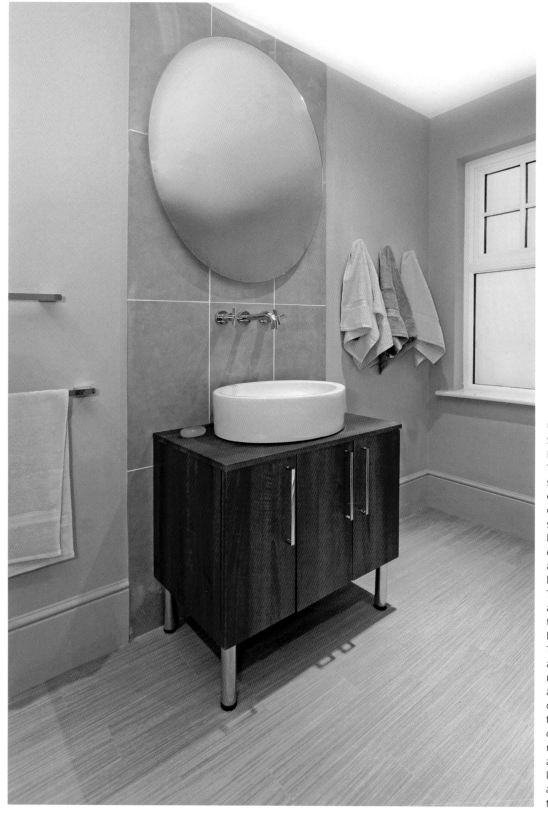

USE BAMBOO FOR SUSTAINABLE, ECONOMICAL FLOORING. Turn to a different sort of floor—and an environmentally friendly choice—by laying bamboo strips or planks in your bathroom. Bamboo floors come in many different appearances depending on how they are manufactured. The grain may appear almost like a hardwood floor or closer and tighter like the floor shown here. The material can be left a light golden brown natural color or tinted in any number of shades and colors. No matter what type of bamboo floor you choose, though, you can rest easy knowing that it's a green choice—although it looks like wood, bamboo is actually a fast-growing grass that is totally sustainable.

USE PLAIN TILES TO GROUND BUSY BATHROOMS. Use large, plain tiles in a large bathroom when you want or need to provide a base for a busy design. The simple neutral tiles in this room are almost two square feet apiece, and the understated look provides some visual relief in a space with lots of lines, different textures, a mix of colors and many different forms. Sometimes, a little plainness can go a long way in a bathroom design.

MIX FLOOR TILES INTO THE WALL TO EXPAND SMALL BATHROOMS. The most common application of mosaic tiles in a bathroom is to run the same tiles from the floor up to the wall. But mix it up for even more visual interest and to serve the needs of the space. In this relatively modest bathroom, the walls are a vibrant blue and white mosaic design, but the white mosaic tiles on the floor not only allow the walls to grab the attention, they also increase the visual size of the space, making a constrained room seem a little more spacious.

Eye-Catching Vanity Counters

MARRY COUNTERS TO OTHER SURFACES. Mix and match your vanity counter successfully to the other surfaces in the room, and the look can be pure magic. Here, a super-colorful counter in polished volcanic stone supplies a burst of color in a bathroom with mirrored walls and white fixtures. It's a fun, dynamic and exciting look in which the surfaces all support one another.

MATCH NATURAL SURFACES TO NATURAL WALL TREATMENTS AND FLOORING. Consider matching natural vanity materials to a natural vanity countertop in your bathroom. The Craftsman-style rough wood vanity here is perfectly paired with a slate counter. Stone vanity surfaces naturally complement wood vanities, especially those stained natural. Slate is just one of many alluring types of stone that could serve well in the bathroom.

MAKE A GLASS COUNTERTOP THE DOMINANT DESIGN FEATURE. You can make a design statement with your vanity counter just as you would with your choice of materials for any of the other dominant surfaces in the space. Here, a cast-glass countertop provides a riveting visual focal point for the room. It offers an incredible surface that invites the brush of a finger and features a unique front edge relief. It's a one-of-a-kind surface that is also durable and easy to clean.

Eye-Catching Vanity Counters

WOOD SLAB COUNTERTOPS COMPLEMENT MANY DIFFERENT STYLES. Establish a contemporary style by using a vessel sink paired with a wood-slab vanity counter. This thick wood vanity surface brings natural graining to the bathroom in a hue that complements the dominant brown color scheme. An interesting variation is used with this vanity: a cylindrical sink has been run right through a hole in the slab, creating an exceptional look that stands out in the room. Another wonderful thing about standalone wood counter vanities like this is that they complement all kinds of sink materials from metal to porcelain.

MATCH THE COUNTERTOP TO OTHER SURFACES TO TIE THE ROOM TOGETHER. Achieve design flow by integrating vanity counters in a material that matches other surfaces in the room. Here, green marble has been used to clad the tub platform, and the counters were crafted in the same marble. It leads the eye around the room and creates design unity. You can use this technique with walls and floors as well.

LAMINATE COUNTERTOPS ARE WORTHWHILE COST-SAVERS. Turn to a laminate countertop for a handsome surface that won't set you back an arm and a leg. Modern laminates come in an incredible range of colors and surface appearances, including the faux-stone look featured here. Although seams in laminate counters can prove problematic, today's laminate surfaces are sealed with incredibly strong adhesives, and the counters are more durable than ever. They are also easy to work with and inexpensive.

SOLID SURFACES ARE CRISP AND CLEAN. Solid-surface countertops are every bit as popular and useful in the bathroom as they are in the kitchen. These materials are colored through and through, which means that scratches can be buffed out on most solid-surface counters. The counter is entirely waterproof, and solid-surface options such as Corian can be molded in one piece with sinks, backsplashes and other features. The icing on the cake is that these materials can be created in a painter's palette of colors and patterns, such as the granite shown here.

Eye-Catching
Vanity Counters

FROSTED GLASS CREATES
A CONTEMPORARY STYLE.
Use frosted tempered float
glass for a vanity surface
that is elegant, refined
and relatively inexpensive.
This one is graced with a
poetically curved porcelain
vessel sink; white sinks are
natural partners to glass
vanity tops. Tempered
glass surfaces such as
this can be made to just
about any size and shape.
The glass is also easy to
clean and completely
waterproof, making it a no-
maintenance surface.

FROSTED GLASS IS SLEEK. Use frosted tempered float glass for a vanity surface that is elegant, refined and relatively inexpensive. This one is graced with a poetically curved porcelain vessel sink; white sinks are natural partners to glass vanity tops, and vessel forms can mean that you don't need any holes in the glass. The glass is also easy to clean and completely waterproof, making it a no-maintenance surface.

TILE A COUNTERTOP AS YOU WOULD A FLOOR. If you love the look of ceramic tile, there's no reason it can't serve as a vanity countertop in your bathroom. Colorful tile such as this is often the best choice for a bathroom, emphasizing the special look of the glazed surface. This vanity counter increases visual interest because the tile has been laid in a diamond pattern. There are plenty of ways to differentiate counter tile from floors and walls.

Beautiful Storage Spaces

Storage is no less important in the bathroom than it is everywhere else in the house. The big difference is that you usually have far less space to work with in a bathroom. No matter how you fit it in, though, bathroom storage solutions should never shortchange style for storage space. Given all the options available, there is simply no reason to make that sacrifice.

Bathroom storage usually centers on the medicine chest and vanity. Smaller bathrooms may not need any storage beyond these two areas (powder rooms may not even need a medicine chest). Whatever the case, choosing a vanity is about balancing what you want to store in it with the type that will best meet the needs of the design.

Larger or busier bathrooms cry out for innovative storage solutions. Often, that translates to wall-mounted cabinets or shelves that don't take up precious floor space but are still totally accessible. Choose a wall-mounted unit to blend in with the vanity and other decorative elements or use it to make a small design statement.

MATCH VANITY TO ROOM STYLE. With so many styles, sizes and types of vanities available, you should have no problem matching one to your particular bathroom design. The vanity in this room is a cool, linear design that suits the room's modern look, and the dark wood finish plays perfectly against the yellow accent wall. A side cabinet in the vanity supplies a nice amount of hidden storage.

Where you require considerable storage space, turn to "suites" of coordinated furniture that give large bathrooms a very polished look (or make your own mix-and-match suite). These days, you'll find bathroom furnishings every bit as stylized and detailed as any crafted for other rooms in the house. Whenever you're outfitting larger rooms, especially master suites, don't be afraid to bring some of the items you'd normally store in a bedroom closet into the bathroom; dress accessories and even underwear can find a place in a large master bathroom with good ventilation and a wealth of storage.

ADD A VANITY COMBINING STORAGE TYPES. Choose a guest-bathroom vanity that has a variety of both open and concealed storage for an amazingly useful addition to the room. A unit such as the one shown here takes up modest space but includes both open shelves and concealed cabinet storage. This vanity provides almost all the storage that you would need in the room. The mix of storage types allows you to display high-style towels and attractive personal care products while hiding away more utilitarian objects such as toilet paper and general cleaning products.

Perfect Vanities

USE RETRACTABLE RACKS TO MAKE VANITIES MORE USEFUL. Make any vanity even more useful with slide-out storage racks. These can hold all kinds of items, and the wire construction is easy to clean in the event of a spill (although you can find solid, slide-out drawers as well). Some vanities and bathroom cabinets come equipped with these types of storage features, but you can easily retrofit your existing undersink or cabinet areas with trays on runners like this one.

CHOOSE A VANITY WITH A MIX OF DRAWERS AND SHELVES IN SHARED BATHROOMS. Always check the interior space carefully when considering which vanity to buy. A mix of drawers and open cabinet space is often the best solution for a shared bathroom, where many different items need to be stored. The option here, with the clean look of a pair of cabinet doors on the front of the vanity and a hidden drawer inside, offers a lot of flexibility in what you can store. Drawers, in particular, go a long way toward keeping odd-shaped bottles, jars and other containers in order.

USE WIDE VANITIES FOR TWO PEOPLE. You can accommodate his-and-her sinks with abundant storage by using a single vanity meant specifically for two users, such as this one. Each sink has its own drawer and dedicated shelf, but the two units are complemented and attached with a central column of drawers that add a lot of storage and create a sharp look. Stainless steel feet are the icing on the cake for a handsome vanity that would work in many different bathroom designs.

CUSTOMIZE VANITY CABINET STORAGE. Make the most of any vanity by equipping it with specialized storage shelves that accommodate your particular needs. Door racks, a special corner shelf, and a tilt-out drawer on top all make this vanity more useful. Choose features like this in a new vanity or as add-ons to retrofit your existing unit, and you'll have taken a big step toward efficiently organizing your bathroom.

MATE SINK STYLE WITH VANITY CONSTRUCTION. Put some thought into the sink you marry with your vanity of choice. Here, a copper vessel sink looks perfect atop a bamboo vanity. The natural materials work great together, but the drawer really shows how suited they are for each other; a slot that divides the drawer allows room for the sink's drainpipe under the vanity's top surface.

Perfect Vanities

MATCH A PAIR OF MIRRORS TO A PAIR OF VANITIES. His-and-her sinks are alluring when paired with his-and-her vanities. This twin setup illustrates just how attractive mirror-image sinks and vanities can be. The matching vanities host square vessel sinks and feature unusual corner handles on the drawers and cabinets, blending into an intriguing cross pattern. The mirrors follow the theme, and their off-center placement echoes the placement of the sinks.

BLEND WALL-MOUNTED AND TRADITIONAL VANITIES IN ONE UNIT. Don't make the mistake of thinking you have to choose between the sleek appearance and open feel of a wall-mounted vanity and the storage you would expect of a traditional style. This unit provides a traditional appearance with loads of hidden and exposed storage—but in a form designed to increase visual space. The floor is left clear, you have storage to spare, and the style is worth writing home about!

VARIED STORAGE TYPES MAKE FOR A USEFUL VANITY. Find a multifaceted vanity such as this and you may start to expand your notion of what should be stored in the bathroom. The central column of drawers provides the opportunity to store what might normally be kept in a bedroom or walk-in closet. This is especially true of a master bath, where the bulk of the dressing is done in the bathroom. You can keep jewelry or accessories in these drawers and free up room in your dresser or even use it store abundant supplies such as bars of soap.

COMBO VANITIES ARE STYLISH SPACE SAVERS. Settle on a great solution for your half-bath by choosing a wall-mounted vanity and mirror combination. This handsome example shows how space-efficient a combination unit can be while still providing plenty of style. A sophisticated white vessel sink paired with a chic and simple faucet sit atop a dark wood unit featuring a single cabinet and tall, narrow mirror. The mirror serves any bathroom well, reflecting an image that includes torso and some lower body, and the entire unit fits in a space narrower than what a toilet would require.

Perfect Vanities

STYLE VANITIES LIKE BEDROOM FURNITURE. Bring the same classic style you might choose for a traditional bedroom suite into your bathroom by choosing an elegantly detailed wood vanity that derives its appearance from period-style furnishings. These two vanities are examples of sophisticated, traditional designs that exhibit all the marks of a fine cabinetmaker's skill and a style full of dignity and subtlety.

REIMAGINE THE VANITY TO ADD AN ARTFUL FEATURE TO THE BATHROOM. It's easy to focus on the function of a vanity and miss the potential to make a design statement with this storage piece. The beautiful wood vanity in this modern bathroom does away with the conventional doors, offering a pleasing composition of shelves in an unexpected, irregular form.

MIRRORED FRONTS ADD GLAMOUR. Add glamour to your bathroom with a vanity featuring mirrored fronts. It's a small design touch that adds immeasurably to the look of the room and just spells fun. This vanity includes a detailed façade with mirrors in every panel. The white marble vanity top doesn't hurt the look either. A little flair in the vanity you choose can bring big design style to a bathroom, small or large.

Handy Cabinets & Shelves

USE VANITIES AS PARTS OF SUITES. For the easiest design, you can find entire suites of bathroom furniture in matching sets at major retailers. A suite of modern pieces creates a harmonious look throughout this guest bathroom. Ebony his-and-her vanities are complemented by a matching central storage tower and wall-mounted tissue dispenser and cube shelf. Notice that even the medicine chest mirrors are styled to match the furniture, with wood bands down the outside of each mirror.

VARY FURNITURE HEIGHTS FOR INCREASED APPEAL. Vary the height of bathroom furnishings to create visual variety and make the room more interesting. The safest way to do this is by using different storage pieces that differ in height but are the same general style, such as the suite used in this bathroom. If the styles and the heights of the pieces vary too much, you start to create visual confusion—the opposite of good design.

CONSERVE FLOOR SPACE WITH WALL-MOUNTED UNITS. Add a wall-hung cabinet to a modest bathroom to create additional storage without taking up valuable floor space. The easiest way to integrate a wall-hung unit like this into the design is to match it to the style of the vanity and mirror. The pieces here all reflect a shaker aesthetic, and small details such as the pulls and corner distressing convince the eye that these pieces are all part of a set—and an attractive set at that.

Handy Cabinets & Shelves

HIDE STORAGE IN WALL-HUNG UNITS. Look to wall-mounted cabinets for space-efficient storage. This example is especially effective, combining abundant storage space behind a flip-up mirrored front panel. It's a sleek design made even sleeker with interior lights and glass shelves. Find storage solutions that work as hard as possible in combining fabulous function with eye-catching form and details.

Handy Cabinets & Shelves

USE FANCY TRIMWORK ON BATHROOM CABINETS. Look for fine details on the storage cabinetry that you select to provide as much style as possible. Many of the storage units available at retail have a completely built-in look that will add something special to the appearance of any bathroom. Signs of skilled craftsmanship shout quality when included in bathroom storage, such as the crown molding top detail, mullioned windows and raised panel cabinet doors shown here.

HANG STORAGE FOR SLEEK, EFFICIENT STYLE. Where your bathroom is space-challenged, turn to the walls to accommodate your storage needs. Get creative with wall-mounted shelving, and you'll often find design solutions in addition to the storage you need. The bamboo shelves that cover the top half of this modest bathroom's wall contain the mirror over the tiny sink and create a bit of design unity, matching the material used to front the bathtub. The light-colored shelving provides abundant storage without visually closing in the space. It's a great, quick-access storage solution that aids the room's look as well.

SAVE SPACE WITH VERTICAL FIXTURES. Follow the trend toward tall, narrow bathroom cabinets to make the most of available space in a small bathroom. This urbane unit is mounted between wall and floor but takes up a minimal footprint. The cabinet can be spun to either side for added convenience and access. The mirrored cabinet door adds to the vanity mirror, and adjustable shelves on the inside make the unit incredibly useful for storing just about anything you might need in the bathroom.

FILL WALL SPACE WITH TOWEL TOWERS. Add a towel tower to an informal family bathroom to keep all the room's textiles in order. Towel clutter is one of the biggest challenges in a busy shared bathroom, and a tower like this provides spaces for lots of towels, as well as bathrobes, shower sponges, bath toys in a bag and more. This tower was custom-built, but you can find prefabricated units at many wood furniture stores (although building them requires only modest skills and basic tools). In addition to all the hanging storage, this tower provides towel drawers and a place to sit.

CREATE DESIGN CONTINUITY. Create continuity in your bathroom's design by using coordinated storage pieces throughout the room. This suite of bathroom furnishings is a perfect example; the pleasing contemporary style mixing dark wood with chrome accents marks the wall-mounted vanity counter, the shelf underneath and a vertical wall-mounted cabinet. The surface-mounted medicine cabinet complements the other pieces, and the total combination of storage ensures that everything has a place, regardless of its size or shape.

HIDE A HAMPER IN YOUR STORAGE. Outfit a busy family bathroom with well-thought-out storage-space customizers to keep the room as shipshape as possible. This pullout, ventilated towel hamper is an incredibly useful feature for holding the wet towels in a busy bathroom while avoiding mold and odor problems. It gives everyone who uses the bathroom an easy place to throw towels when they're done, and it hides towels awaiting laundry, keeping the space looking neat at all times.

SEPARATE HIS-AND-HER SINKS WITH A STORAGE COLUMN. Position a storage column between his-and-her sinks to create a sense of separation and add significant shared storage to the room. This column is a great example, running from the vanity counter up to the ceiling. It clearly defines the two different sink areas and lends accessible storage to both sinks. Notice how the column is complemented by a bump-out drawer unit that also serves to separate the two sink areas.

Handy Cabinets & Shelves

STORE EVERYTHING IN A HUTCH. You can turn to an all-in-one bathroom hutch to provide all the storage a bathroom could need. This unit is typical of the high-end, full-height units available, featuring an assortment of cabinet sizes and shapes, concealing both shelves and drawers. The styles on the market range from the traditional, like this unit, to much more modern and streamlined pieces.

FLOATING SHELVES ARE SIMPLE, STYLISH STORAGE SOLUTIONS. Add a bit of flair to any bathroom—regardless of the design style—with floating shelves. The shelves fool the eye because the mounting brackets are not visible. These can be positioned on most any wall in the room and are wonderful complements to standalone cabinetry. The shelves are ideally suited for the fairly lightweight items commonly stored in a bathroom. Pretty bottles and jars, colorful hand towels and handsome makeup boxes can all find a home on floating shelves.

KEEP THE LOOK SLEEK WITH GLASS SHELVING. Spruce up the look of any sink or toilet area with the addition of a nicely styled glass shelf. Glass shelves like this—sometimes called "vanity" shelves—provide a clean and airy appearance with little visual weight. This particular shelf is perfectly placed to hold personal care products used at the sink. It's also got a bit of style, boasting a chic chrome front rail and chrome mounts that match the faucet and the towel bar brackets. It's an extremely pulled-together look.

USE THE WALL AS A BUILT-IN SHELF. As this ultra-modern bathroom shows, you can literally build-in a shelving substitute. If you're tiling an entire wall, like the wall behind this bathtub, it's not hard to frame in a stepped knee wall in front of the main wall, creating a ledge that is much longer and stronger than most wall-mounted shelves. Although this ledge is used to hold towels and other light items, it could just as easily be used to store heavier things.

Handy Cabinets & Shelves

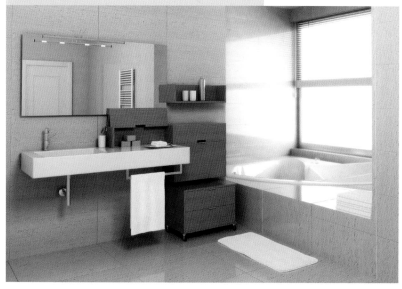

PORTABLE BATHROOM STORAGE ADDS FUNCTION AND FORM. Use a rolling cabinet to double as handy storage and a portable table. The small rolling storage pictured here complements the vanity and wood accents in the room, but it also provides a top surface for drinks or candles to be enjoyed during a long, leisurely bath. It could also be used to hold a pile of magazines or the personal care products that don't find a place on the vanity counter.

USE RECESSED STORAGE IN TIGHT QUARTERS. Where space is tight, turn to a recessed cabinet for plenty of storage without biting into the bathroom's floor plan. Building in one of these incredibly handy storage features is not a difficult project, and it gives you the chance to add to the room's style. You can include drawers, cabinets and open shelving in recessed units such as this—choose the type of storage based on what you most need to store there.

USE STORAGE AS DECORATION. Be creative when coming up with storage solutions in a bathroom because the best examples use attractive items in unique ways, turning what needs to be stored into decorative accents. Here, a wide, skinny box shelf has been used as a place for extra towels. By storing the towels rolled up, the feature becomes a design element. Towels are especially good candidates for "decorative" storage.

MIX PULL-OUT RACKS AND SOLID SHELVES IN HIDDEN STORAGE. Always look at storage as an opportunity to style your bathroom. This clean country-style built-in cabinet not only provides a wealth of storage space for the bathroom it serves, it also adds an attractive decorative element. Notice that the cabinet is equipped with shelves at many different heights, as well as slick slide-out trays on runners that keep uniquely shaped bottles, jars and odds and ends in order. Equip hidden storage with these kinds of specialized features, and you make the storage even more useful than it normally would be.

Bathing in Style

The diverse types, styles and designs of bathtubs and showers are simply mind-boggling. Today's bathing structures range from basic functional units that fit neatly in an existing spot to incredible standalone tubs and freestanding shower enclosures that can best be described as works of art. There truly is a bathtub or shower for every style of bathroom.

However, searching for the perfect tub usually starts with pragmatic concerns. Any tub you choose will most likely need to fit into an existing space, positioned to take advantage of the plumbing's location. Even if you're working within these constraints, the available options are amazingly varied. You'll find beautiful alcove tubs with special features such as lights, molded seats and built-in decks, and prefab alcove shower enclosures that look custom-made.

On the other hand, if you're completely remodeling your bathroom or building new, the sky's the limit. A shower with multiple heads, steam fittings and a bench seat can transform a morning ritual into an exhilarating experience. A deep soaking tub shaped like Cinderella's slipper can turn a simple bathroom into a relaxing and restorative sanctuary.

Regardless of whether you're looking for a handsome neo-angle shower to fit into the corner of a smaller bathroom or want a two-person whirlpool tub to take center stage in a luxurious master bathroom, the tub or shower should always reflect the bathroom's style and your own tastes. No matter which you choose though, there's no reason you can't have a beautiful design element that erases the tension and dust of the day like magic.

USE CORNER ENCLOSURES WHEN SPACE IS TIGHT. Whenever possible, you'll make your bathroom a lot more usable if you can engineer a floor plan that includes both a bathtub and a shower. Often, the best solution is a corner enclosure such as the one used here. Constructed of frameless glass panels, this enclosure maintains the open, airy feeling established by the soaring ceilings and skylight.

COLOR YOUR BATHTUB TO MATCH YOUR BATHROOM. Add a little color to your bathroom by choosing a freestanding bathtub with a tinted body. A tub such as this brings plenty of seductive form to a room, but the muted color is a nice added touch that complements the room's color scheme and makes the showcase whirlpool tub even more of a standout. This particular tub is an interesting model, containing the motors and plumbing for the jets within the streamlined body—most whirlpool tubs are drop-in style, meant to be used with a larger enclosure. A tub like this allows for that same luxury without requiring the fuss of a custom-built platform.

Gorgeous Freestanding Bathtubs

MATCH A COPPER TUB TO WOOD FLOORS. When you decide on a freestanding tub, you can pick from lots of unique looks. This tub is one example of the distinctive styles available. With an exterior surface clad in copper leaf and a deep porcelain interior, the tub would be right at home in a country-style bathroom or even a contemporary room.

SITE YOUR TUB ATOP UNEXPECTED FLOORING. Do your tastes run to the unusual in tub finishes? Freestanding tubs may answer your desires because many are crafted in unusual materials. This tub, for instance, is brushed nickel and made from recycled materials. It's a completely unique look that seems right at home on a bed of river rocks. Don't limit yourself to white porcelain, because so many more options are available to the open-eyed tub shopper.

SUSPEND YOUR TUB IN A STYLISH FRAME. Go contemporary with an updated version of the traditional clawfoot tub. This bathtub is a drop-in unit suspended in an interesting wood frame with silver feet. It's a subtle and contemporary take on the classic footed tub, one that works well with a contemporary design scheme. Finding unusual and visually arresting alternatives to classic fixture designs is a great way to personalize a bathroom and make it a showcase.

RETROFIT PERIOD FIXTURES TO NEWER TUBS. You can even find colored versions like the clawfoot tub in this bathroom at high-end suppliers and firms that supply renovated period fixtures. You can also purchase an older tub from a salvage vendor and paint it whatever color suits the room. Just be sure to use special paint made specifically for cast iron or whatever material your tub is crafted from.

Gorgeous Freestanding Bathtubs

USE ODD SHAPES IN MODERN-STYLED ROOMS. Select a high-end freestanding tub for its sculptural beauty as well as for the luxurious bathing experience. As this egg-shaped tub shows, some freestanding units are almost lyrical in their form and can transform a bathroom design. This one is right at home in a modern bathroom, where it pops out against the ebonized floor and contrasts the linear forms in the space. It's no slouch when it comes time for a bath, either; the tub is deep and perfectly shaped for a long, comfortable soak.

MIX THE OLD WITH THE NEW. You can choose a bathtub for its classic style, but always keep an eye out for modern conveniences and luxuries common to today's freestanding tubs. This clawfoot tub looks like it could have stepped right out of a hundred-year-old bathroom, except that it is equipped with levelers in each of the feet, and it's paired with a state-of-the-art freestanding faucet assembly that includes a handheld showerhead. Luxury and classic looks all in one package make for a pretty picture.

SPOTLIGHT SHOWCASE TUBS. Make a freestanding tub every bit the centerpiece that drop-in whirlpool tubs—with their substantial platforms and decks—often are. This tub has been situated in an alcove of its own with an impressive column of designer tiles rising up behind it. Detailed silver feet distinguish the fixture, and a rainwater head complements the tub faucet and completes what is surely the centerpiece of this bathroom.

Gorgeous
Freestanding Bathtubs

ELEVATE A BEAUTIFUL TUB. When you've gone through the trouble of seeking out a very special tub—such as this deep pedestal tub with its unusual matte finish—consider showcasing it by putting it on its own stage. Here, the tub sits on an inlaid surface of stone that complements the stunning stacked flagstone wall behind the tub. Even the lights serve to emphasize the tub's simple yet engaging form.

Gorgeous Freestanding Bathtubs

USE CHAIRS AS TUB TABLES. When you've settled on a freestanding pedestal or footed tub, always try to fit some sort of useful side table surface—here, the seat of this chair—into the room's design. The one drawback to freestanding tubs is that they have no deck or lip on which to rest shampoo, soap, candles or any of the other small items that traditionally find a place around a tub. By adding a small table, stool, chair or other surface, you make the tub more practical and, consequently, more comfortable.

SHOWCASE UNIQUE TUBS. The more distinctive the tub, the more you should consider making it a centerpiece of the room's design. Here, an antiqued copper pedestal tub has been placed in the middle of the room, resting on a handsome hardwood floor. The tub's finish fits right in with the floor's stain and makes the fixture the riveting visual star of the show.

Gorgeous Freestanding Bathtubs

VARY TUB COLOR FOR EYE-CATCHING EFFECTS. It may be the most popular look, but don't feel locked into choosing a white bathtub. If your bathroom design is better suited to another hue, you'll find tubs in off-white, brown, and black, like the one in this room. A black tub can be stunning, especially when coupled with other black decorative elements, such as the marble-tile floor in this room. This particular tub features gold-colored feet and faucet fittings, a wonderful touch that makes the tub appear even more sumptuous.

WHITE COMPLEMENTS A WIDE RANGE OF STYLES. Choose an unassuming contemporary freestanding tub style for a fixture that will be appropriate for bathroom styles from country to modern. This unassuming yet elegant bathtub has been positioned in a large dressing room of a summer house but would be just as at home in a marble-clad, minimal modern bathroom. A tub with a form that is this adaptable is unlikely to ever become dated or need replacement.

Gorgeous Alcove Bathtubs

USE APRONS AS DECORATIVE FEATURES. Spruce up the look of a simple alcove tub with a unique apron finish. The front surfaces of these types of tubs are most often left white, but that's not a hard-and-fast rule. You can inject a jolt of color or pattern on the apron. Here, a black apron contrasts the white and faux wood surfaces elsewhere in the room and increases the visual interest of the overall design. You'll find aprons in wood textures, colors, stone looks and more.

MATCH TUB SHAPE TO AVAILABLE SPACE. Choose a bathtub shape to optimize the available space. Here, an oval tub fits neatly into a standard alcove, but because the front edge of the tub bulges out, the interior capacity of the tub is appreciably greater than normal. It's a great way to incorporate a soaking or whirlpool tub without having to structurally change your entire bathroom layout. The unibody design of this tub makes it easy to install in the space, alleviating the need to construct a separate deck.

Gorgeous
Alcove Bathtubs

LOOK FOR APRONS WITH FLAIR. Don't assume that having an alcove tub means a plain, flat-front design. As this tub demonstrates, you can find extraordinary tubs to fit in whatever size slot you have available in your bathroom. This model includes a bowl shape that allows for more spacious bathing than most alcove tubs and an interesting apron design that brings its own life to the design party.

Gorgeous
Alcove Bathtubs

TILE THE TUB APRON. Make your alcove bathtub special by tiling the front apron. This tub pops out of its alcove with a vibrant mosaic tile surface that plays on a border that runs around the tiled walls. Because the surface of an apron juts out from the walls, you can use a radically different tile shape or style on an apron, and the look will still work, as long as the colors don't clash.

FRAME YOUR DROP-IN WITH A DECK. Dress up a plain apron alcove tub by cradling it in a sumptuous deck. The basic tub here is made spectacular with the help of luxury stone deck crafted from the same material as the tile floor. The stone is an ideal tub surround material, and the modest exposure of edging and façade means the luxury surface didn't set the homeowner back an arm and a leg. This is a great way to make a plain feature pop.

Gorgeous
Alcove Bathtubs

WRAP AN ALCOVE TUB IN TILE. Add a distinguished allure to an otherwise undistinguished tub shape by tiling around an alcove tub with high-quality stone tile. The marble tile used on the walls around this tub makes for an eye-catching surface. By covering the front apron in the same tile, the homeowner has blended the simple shape of the tub into the stunning backdrop.

GO SIMPLE AND STRONG. Sometimes it's best to let the simple elegance of an alcove tub stand on its own. This tub features a modest design element in the relief on the apron, but otherwise, the tub perfectly matches the other fixtures in the room, allowing the stone-tiled walls to be the stars of the show.

Gorgeous Corner Bathtubs

CONSERVE ROOM WITH A CORNER TUB. Saving space is perhaps the most compelling reason to choose a corner tub. The front arc of this unit allows for a much wider lane of travel through the room and can make a big difference in the small floor plan of most bathrooms. Of course, as this unit shows, the flowing shape of a corner bathtub is also appealing to the eye; most corner tubs are manufactured to maintain a large capacity even though they're configured for corner placement.

ROUNDED CORNER TUBS EASE NAVIGATION. Tight spaces call for a corner bath with a rounded shape, such as this one. Every little bit helps in opening up a lane of travel in a constricted bathroom floor plan. The bonus is that the shape of the tub is informal and inviting, and the pure white color and simple lines visually calm down what is a fairly busy room design.

SITE FOR LIGHT. Position a corner tub correctly and you can take advantage of the light from a window without exposing any part of the tub—and any bather in it—to the outside view. This tub is perfectly positioned in relation to the window. In addition, the front apron of the tub is colored to match the wall, so that it recedes visually and seems more of an integral part of the room.

POSITION TUB FAUCETS FOR BATHING COMFORT. A naturally pleasing visual order can be found when you place the faucet at the rear of a corner tub, as it has been here. It can also make getting in and out of the tub much easier than if the spout is mounted along the front. The back ledge is also handy for storing bathing products or toys for a child's bath—one of the advantages of a corner bathtub is the abundant ledge space.

USE TIERS IN YOUR DROP-IN. Are you pining for ultimate luxury in your master bath? Where you have the room, indulge your inner hedonist with an over-the-top spa bath like this one. Featuring dozens of adjustable jets, molded back rests and body stalls, lights and temperature controls, this tub provides a one-of-a-kind bathing experience. It also shines on the style front with a hardwood ledge and sleek faucet. A tub like this deserves to be the centerpiece around which a bathroom is designed, as is the case here. A backlit transparent wall, a row of plants and custom step-up deck all give the bathtub top billing.

CHOOSE UNDERMOUNT TUBS FOR SUBTLER LOOKS. If you aren't fond of the drop-in look, but you want to install a large whirlpool tub in your bathroom, you can turn to an undermount version such as this. The tub sits under a deck, just as an undermount sink does. This position minimizes the look of the tub's lip, and allows you to create a deck in any material that suits your design and tastes. The wood here has been finished top and bottom to ensure against moisture infiltration and provides a wonderful warm and comfortable top surface for getting in and out of the tub.

EMBELLISH DECKS WITH BORDERS OF FINE TRIMWORK OR STONE. Take the opportunity of building a surround for your drop-in whirlpool bathtub to create a unique, scene-setting feature. This tub has been framed in an enclosure that includes a river-rock border inside the tub's deck. It's a naturalistic look that complements the wood deck and the plants used in the room, and it gives the bather the sense of dipping into a serene stream. Special, innovative features such as this give you an opportunity to put your fingerprints on a bathroom design.

Gorgeous Drop-In Bathtubs

TWO-PERSON TUBS OFFER SUMPTUOUS COUPLE LUXURY. Carry through on the theme of a his-and-her bathroom by installing a drop-in tub for two. A tub such as this one provides luxury bathing for two people at the same time. The tub echoes the his-and-her sinks and mirrors and defines the space as an opulent bathroom dedicated to a sensual experience for two, far beyond mere bathing.

ADD STEPS FOR ACCESSIBILITY AND STYLE. Make any drop-in tub more accessible by adding a step alongside the platform. This marble platform is incredibly opulent, and the step adds visual interest around the tub. More importantly, it increases safety, making it easier for bathers to get in and out of the tub without slipping. Even low platforms can benefit from the addition of a step. If you prefer, switch up the design and craft a step out of a different material than the tub platform itself.

INCORPORATE FINE DETAILS. If you're going to the trouble to build a detailed drop-in tub platform, you might as well go the extra mile and make the platform a distinct design focal point in and of itself. The platform built to hold this round tub is not only an enchanting hardwood surface finished natural, but it also has been designed with a series of indented steps that add lines, angles and usability to the look. The platform is accented by fascinating inlays on the apron, with matching designs on the step risers. It's a powerful presence in a modest bathroom.

Gorgeous Drop-In Bathtubs

MAKE THE DROP-IN THE CENTERPIECE. Create an incredibly inviting scene in your master bathroom by positioning a whirlpool tub as the centerpiece of the room. The drop-in unit dominates this lovely bathroom; the stylish tiled surround contains the heater and motor elements for the tub. The tub itself features both air and water jets, a range of settings, interior colored lights, and a specially molded shape to cradle the bather's body in ultimate luxury. Add a tub like this to your bathroom and you may just forget you don't live at a luxury spa.

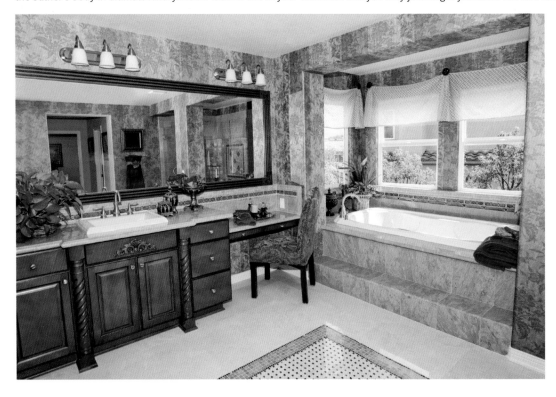

MATCH LARGE DROP-INS TO LARGE SPACES. If your alcove is large, there's no sense settling for a simple alcove tub. Here, a sizeable window alcove is filled with a modest step-up platform housing a standard rectangular drop-in tub. The tub sits conveniently next to a makeup area, creating a fluid interchange between bathing and dressing.

TUCK DROP-IN TUBS IN CORNERS. Corners can be the perfect location for a drop-in tub. As this installation shows, a corner orientation leaves plenty of tub deck on which you can place hair-care and body-care products, candles, washcloths and whatever else you need to keep around the tub. The angle also allows more room to navigate around the tub, and an oval-shaped bathtub is perfect for the installation. A leaded-glass window is an elegant bonus.

USE A PENINSULA TUB TO BREAK UP A LONG ROOM. A drop-in tub placed in a peninsula jutting out from a wall is a great way to section off a larger bathroom. This configuration makes the tub the star of the room and creates distinct areas on either side that you can dedicate to dressing, makeup or other functions. This mottled stone tub deck and copious candles used as accents help focus attention on the peninsula shape.

CHOOSE A TUB FOR COUPLES. His-and-her luxury, drop-in whirlpool tubs are becoming increasingly popular, and you can create your own intimate couples spa experience by adding one of these bathtubs to your bathroom. This model is relatively narrow, it fits well into a constricted space next to an expansive shower enclosure. The molded seats, complete with seat backs, are formed to allow comfortable reclining and ultimate bathing in a modicum of room.

ENRICH SHOWERING WITH A LARGE ENCLOSURE. Exploit large bathroom spaces and make showering more luxurious by expanding the shower enclosure to fill an available open area. The large footprint of a shower such as this makes the morning (or evening) wash-down an unrivaled pleasure, and the combination of stone mosaic and large square tiles is simply jaw-dropping. Adding a bench is almost a must in a large shower, and you can build one in as the designer did here or add a waterproof portable shower stool or bench.

BLEND AN ENCLOSURE INTO THE ROOM'S STYLE. Make sure your shower enclosure design is appropriate to the overall bathroom style. Although it's tempting to view the enclosure as a chance for design fireworks in the bathroom, sometimes it's wise to be more subdued. The elegant, restrained, light and airy look of this room called for an enclosure that blends in rather than stands out. The frameless glass doors are perfect for the light-filled space, and the shower faucet matches the bidet and vanity faucets. It's a perfectly unified design that's pleasing to the eye.

INSTALL EDGE DRAINS TO INCREASE COMFORT. Always try to minimize the impact of the drain on how comfortable the shower is to stand in. Center drains are the easiest to install, but they can make for a canted floor that is uncomfortable over the course of long, steamy showers—and who wants to take a short shower? This drain system runs along the edge of the floor, and needs only a slight gradient to effectively drain off shower water. It's a streamlined and sophisticated design decision.

Luxury Shower
Enclosures

USE IDENTICAL BATHROOM SURFACES IN YOUR SHOWER ENCLOSURE. Consider replicating stunning surfaces used elsewhere in the bathroom in your shower enclosure. The stone tiles used for the floor in this bathroom were also used as a tub surround and then run into and up the walls of the shower enclosure. Not only is the material inherently spectacular, but using it in this way also creates incredible visual continuity that ties together the entire bathroom design. Note that the larger tiles have been used throughout; large tiles look more appropriate in large bathrooms than smaller sizes would.

SHOWER CURTAINS ARE ALSO LUXURIOUS. Who says a shower enclosure has to be a freestanding, separate construction? In keeping with the period look of this footed tub, the shower is run up from the Victorian-style faucet fittings with a period-appropriate shower curtain ring. The shower includes a luxury head with porcelain lip and a handheld head with its own diverter controls. It's a lot of shower luxury in a small amount of space and keeps the distinctive look of the room in perfect order.

Luxury Shower Enclosures

SIMPLIFY FOR A CALMING EFFECT. Nothing says you need to make a big bang with your shower enclosure. Sometimes, simpler is better. The solid blue mosaic tile covering the walls and floor of this shower stall give it a calm, lovely aspect. The tile was also easier to install in straight lines and right angles than it would have been on curving surfaces or to execute a highly detailed tile pattern. The look is plain but beautiful and low key.

SAVE SPACE WITH NEO SHOWERS. Fit a freestanding shower into your modest bathroom by using a neo-round enclosure. These types of enclosures often come as kits, with shower pan, glass door and panels, and all the hardware included. This pivot door opens both ways to make it easy to use the shower, and some neo enclosures come with bypass doors that slide or roll on tracks, making them even more space efficient. All the same, these kits don't have to look like a kit. As this shower shows, a tiny, neo-round shower can be a style high point in the bathroom.

CORNER SHOWERS SUIT TIGHT FLOOR PLANS. Build-in a corner shower to take advantage of otherwise unused floor space and create a luxury element in a tight fit. This corner shower is fluidly blended with the mosaic and the rest of the room, sharing the same green brick tile. A frameless, clear-glass enclosure ensures that the space remains visually open and airy and that natural light makes its way into the shower.

Luxury Shower Enclosures

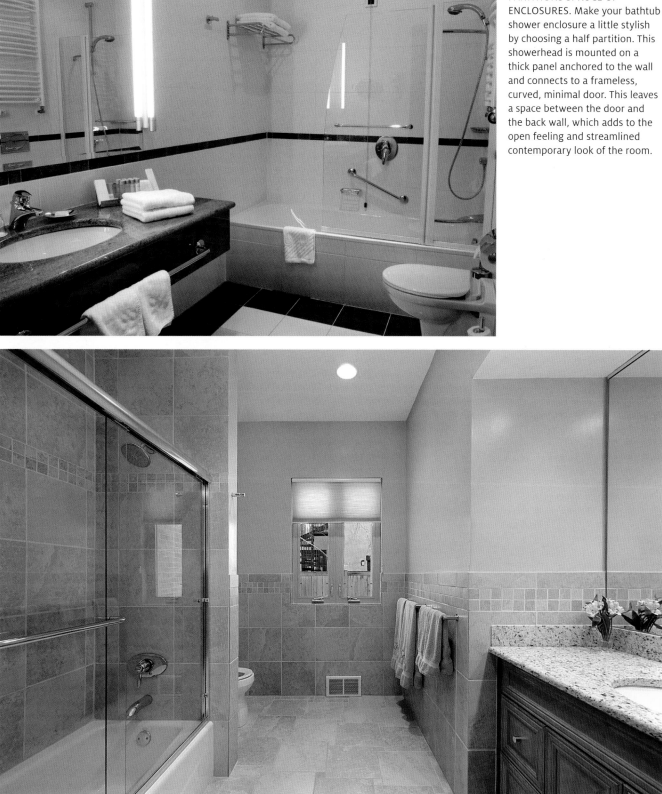

PARTITIONS SPRUCE UP ENCLOSURES. Make your bathtub shower enclosure a little stylish by choosing a half partition. This showerhead is mounted on a thick panel anchored to the wall and connects to a frameless, curved, minimal door. This leaves a space between the door and the back wall, which adds to the open feeling and streamlined contemporary look of the room.

SAVE SPACE WITH SLIDING DOORS. Bypass tub-and-shower doors conserve space and completely contain shower water. Bypass doors like these are the most common style used on bathtub showers. It's a cleaner look than a shower curtain, and the doors come in variety of potential glass styles from perfectly clear to slightly opaque textured to entirely opaque frosted glass. They are easy to install with minimal skills and effort.

Luxury Shower Enclosures

BUILT-IN SHELVES ADD DESIGN PIZZAZZ AND USABLE SPACE. Make any shower enclosure easier to use by adding cutouts when constructing the enclosure. This particular cutout is even more interesting in that the shower control has been located inside. The ledge is useful for holding soap, loofahs, other sundries, or just decorative touches such as the seashells exhibited in this shower. Cutouts are typically tiled, not only to match the enclosure's walls, but also to prevent water infiltration.

USE CURTAINS TO EASILY CHANGE YOUR SHOWER DESIGN. Although glass shower doors are common upgrades for bathtub showers, nothing says you can't make a style statement with a simple bath curtain. This plain curtain complements the brown tones and stone surfaces of the bath and shower and functions nicely in place of a door. Using a curtain also gives you a chance to change up the look at a whim; you can choose from an incredible number of shower curtain designs, and most are inexpensive.

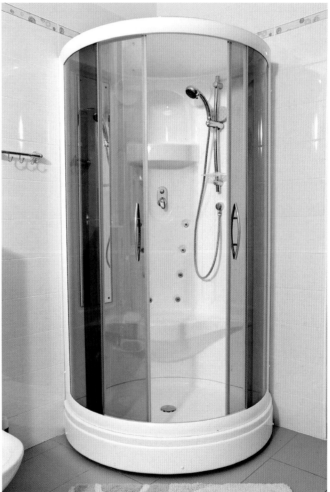

FINE-TUNE SHOWER STYLE WITH HARDWARE PLACEMENT. Put your own stamp on a simple bathtub shower by how you detail the space. Here, a handheld shower has been installed instead of a more static showerhead, and the controls for the shower have been routed to the side wall, rather than placed above the bath controls. The soap dish and corner shelf are coordinated so that the brushed steel look of the fixtures is carried throughout the shower. It's a simple, clean and elegant look.

COMPACT ENCLOSURES CAN ALSO BE LUXURIOUS, APPEALING AND FUN. When it comes to prefab shower enclosures, you don't have to give up style and luxury features to save a little space. This compact round corner shower occupies a tiny footprint in the bathroom but packs a big punch when it comes to enjoyable decadence. The enclosure features a sliding bypass door, a molded-in seat, multiple shower spray heads, a handheld head and a steam feature. That's more than you might find in a much bigger custom enclosure!

Luxury Shower Enclosures

FRAMED DOORS OFFER TRADITIONAL LOOKS. Keep your shower simple with a traditional framed shower door. If your alcove shower opening is wide enough, you can use one of these simple hinged doorsets, which come complete and ready to install. The look is traditional and conventional, but with clear panels in place, it leaves a wide-open view to show off special shower tile designs, such as the walls and floor in this alcove.

MIX SIMPLE DOORS WITH BUSY WALLS. Although framed bypass shower doors may be considered a stodgy look in some quarters, you can make them part of a sleek bathroom design by backing them with a stunning shower surround. The sophisticated tile covering the walls in this shower offers big visual pop and makes the clean lines and clear glass of the shower doors seem streamlined and almost modern. Always consider any design element against all the rest in the bathroom before making a final judgment.

FRAMELESS STYLE IS SUPER SLEEK. It's hard to go wrong when you craft your shower enclosure with frameless glass panels. These are fairly easy to install, sexy to behold and suit just about any style of bathroom. You can also find a fantastic range of sizes to accommodate shower stalls, large and small. Where a solid-wall enclosure might block light coming into the room, a glass cube allows for maximum light penetration.

Superb Fixtures

Sinks, toilets and bidets are functional fixtures that actually define a bathroom's purpose, but they are also elements of the room's style. As such, they can be simple background pieces in the greater "picture" of the room—as most toilets are—or they can be design highlights—as many modern sinks are.

Toilets and the European-import bidets are limited in terms of design flair. The sitting fixtures in a bathroom are really more about function than anything else. They must, however, blend nicely into the design. Although people rarely make a design statement with their choice of toilet or bidet, you will find a variety of tank types, from low-slung contemporary versions to interesting cylindrical models.

There is far more sexy potential in the many sink options on the market. First off, you'll be choosing from four basic styles: drop-in, pedestal or console, wall-mount and vessel. Drop-ins are the most common, being used with a vanity. Vessels are the newest form. But every style of sink comes in a mind-boggling range of materials, finishes and forms.

Choose the sink or sinks that help define the look and feel you're after while still accommodating the people who use the room. Choose new toilets and bidets to support the rest of the elements in the room, and you'll have the perfect mix of fixtures for your bathroom design.

USE SIMPLE TOILETS IN LAVISH SETTINGS. When you've gone to the trouble of cladding your bathroom surfaces in a magnificent material such as gold tile, you may want to minimize the appearance of the functional toilet and bidet. Here, simple streamlined wall-mounted units serve the purpose perfectly without stealing any attention from the incredible surroundings.

GO DEMURE WITH A WALL-MOUNTED TOILET. Wall-mounted toilets have become popular in recent years because they minimalize the visual impact of a fixture that most people do not want to showcase. In any case, the streamlined form is a nice one, and a wall-mounted toilet may be just right for you, especially if you've opted for a darker bathroom color scheme, such as the deep brown in this room. The bright white of the sink and toilet prevent the overall scene from becoming too heavy and closed in.

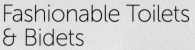

CLASSIC TOILET STYLE ALWAYS WORKS. Choose a classic-style toilet for a room with traditional, ornate tile work. A fixture like this has enough panache in the curves of its form to hold its own against a background of detailed tile work in multiple shapes and shades, and the bright white finish is classic. What's more, a long, sturdy grab bar makes this particular feature more accessible.

BASIC TOILET FORMS COMPLEMENT MODERN ROOM STYLES. A toilet does not necessarily have to be low-slung and futuristic to work well in a modern bathroom design. This simple two-piece toilet has an elegant and timeless look, with a modestly flared tank (along with a high-powered flush capability to prevent clogs). The flat tank top provides additional storage space akin to a small shelf, and the bright white finish works perfectly with the patterned wallpaper and plush, richly colored textiles.

CHOOSE VINTAGE FIXTURES WITH MODERN TECHNOLOGY. Have a hankering for vintage luxury style? Some bath fixture manufacturers cater to the restoration ideal, offering fixtures like this vintage overhead-tank toilet and bidet reproduction. The fixtures look like those of yesteryear, but the actual plumbing is updated to meet today's stricter water-use regulations and powerful flush capability. It's the best of the past and present, all in a stylish look that's hard to beat.

ACCENT TOILETS WITH HARDWARE. Accessorize toilets and bidets with high-end faucets and hardware. The expense is relatively modest, but the boost to your bathroom's design is extravagant. This is a great place to incorporate really distinctive materials that you might not use throughout the bathroom, such as the gold fittings shown here. The fittings and other essential accessories (such as the toilet brush set) give you a chance to add vivid color, unusual materials or one-of-kind finishes without overwhelming the room's design.

GET EUROPEAN WITH A TANKLESS TOILET. You need to have the right type of plumbing, but where you do, you can install a tankless, pressure-assist toilet. This toilet has a distinctly European look and complements the bidet perfectly. It's also a natural partner to this bistro-style aesthetic, created with checkerboard flooring and simple wood-framed mirrors over the fixtures.

Fashionable Toilets & Bidets

DEFINE SIGNATURE ROOM STYLE WITH TOILET FORM. Use an unusually shaped toilet for an arresting, original statement in your bathroom. A style such as this, with a nearly square tank and back, can be an endlessly interesting addition to your bathroom design. Because the seat of a toilet can only range so much in size and shape and still accommodate its function, style variations usually play out in the tank. This one is cool and sophisticated.

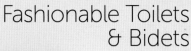

Fashionable Toilets & Bidets

MATCH THE FORM OF ALL FIXTURES. Create a coolly coordinated look in your bathroom by choosing fixtures with matching styling. This bathroom is outfitted with a toilet that seems formed from the same mold as the sink and tub. All three feature a curvy, simple and attractive look. You can establish a strong design theme with fixtures this closely matched.

RESTRAIN WITH WHITE FORMS AND FIXTURES. Don't be afraid to go mono-color in your bathroom, especially if the color is white. Because of its association with cleanliness, white is the perfect choice for a bathroom, and it creates a calm, uncluttered appeal for smaller rooms. A plain, mono-color scheme calls for a plain, simple toilet such as this one. This bathroom shows how attractive a bit of restraint can be.

Chic Sink Colors

COLOR THE BATHROOM WITH A SINK. Think twice before jumping at that pure white sink on display; there are myriad other sink color options from which to choose. Although white is the most popular and common color, off-whites and beiges work equally well in a range of bathroom designs. Faux stone surface appearances are also a great choice for a range of different room styles. Of course, you can go a bit wilder too.

Chic Drop-In Sinks

CHOOSE THE UNUSUAL FOR A STANDARD DROP-IN. Don't fall into the trap of thinking a drop-in sink needs to be staid. You have many of the same options in drop-in units as you do in vessel sinks. The hammered copper sink in this vanity is just one example. The surface is fascinating to behold and equally fascinating to touch. By choosing matching faucets, the homeowner has created a nicely unified look and even helped the environment—this sink is made from recycled materials.

ROUND AND WHITE IS TIMELESS. Go classic with a round or oval white porcelain sink. The traditional style involves pairing the sink with chrome fixtures, a combination that complements almost any style of bathroom design. White porcelain sinks always look clean and bright, and they always look great with other decorative features, like this intricate backsplash tile.

Chic Drop-In Sinks

COMPLEMENT THE VANITY. The design of a drop-in sink most often takes its cue from the style set by the vanity. This hand-hammered sink offers an incredibly detailed rough-hewn finish that matches the wood vanity and antiqued faucet, as well as the brighter copper frame on the mirror. As distinctive as it might be, every bathroom sink is part of a grouping of design elements that must work together.

UNDERMOUNTS ARE CLEAN AND SEAMLESS. An alternative version of the drop-in sink, the undermount creates a cleaner look for the vanity counter. As this elegant bathroom vanity shows, the undermount sink lets the countertop—in this case, marble—grab all the attention. Undermount sinks also have a practical side, because they make cleanup easier; the lack of a lip allows you to simply wipe water or dirt into the sink.

UNDERMOUNT SINKS CAN BE DRAMATIC. Moderate the power of an extremely distinctive sink by using an undermount version; the one-of-kind surface treatment is revealed only as a person approaches the vanity. This brushed nickel sink with its hammered "petal" bowl design is spectacular, perfectly matched with a brushed nickel faucet. The plain white countertop allows the sink to dazzle close up and keeps it from overwhelming the bathroom's aesthetic from other vantage points in the room.

CREATE VISUAL SURPRISE WITH A SINK. When it comes to bathroom sinks, think outside the confines of the vanity countertop if you want to make a truly surprising and original design statement. This nickel sink is an undermount version of a drop-in form, but with a twist: it has a front apron that projects out of a cutout in the front edge of the counter. This is obviously a special installation, but one that never lacks for attention.

Chic Drop-In Sinks

SQUARE SINKS OFFER MORE ROOM. Use a square drop-in sink on a wider or square vanity top, especially where you want a sink with more room inside. This sink features edge detailing that adds a little flair to an otherwise basic white porcelain fixture. Notice that the homeowner has decided to use faucets with an antiqued style that complements the sink nicely.

APRON SINKS PROVIDE THE UNEXPECTED. Turn to an apron drop-in sink for an unusual and entirely different look in your bathroom. This style nests in an alcove in the vanity and appears very substantial. It helps if the sink is a weighty material, such as the hammered copper shown here, but enameled cast iron or even a hefty porcelain unit will work. You'll need to have the right type of vanity, though; one thick enough to accommodate the height of the apron.

Chic Wall-Mount Sinks

ADD A BACKDROP TO WALL-MOUNT SINKS. Make your wall-mount sink sing by using a half-height wall covering behind it. The wall surface acts almost as a canvas, emphasizing the style of the sink. However, if you use this design technique, it's best if the plumbing is concealed; this sink is formed with a trap cover as part of the sink's body. It's also a good idea to use accents that complement the sink, such as the sleek faucet, soap tray and towel ring included here.

CHOOSE WALL-MOUNTS FOR DIVERSITY. Pick a wall-mount sink for the space-saving aspects, and you can choose from among an incredible diversity of styles. Looks range from sedate contemporary styles to extreme country versions. This half-barrel wall-mounted vanity is topped with a single-surface hammered-copper counter and sink. The look isn't right for every bathroom, but in the right style of home, it makes an impressive statement.

HIDE THE PLUMBING. Don't shy away from choosing a wall-mount sink just because you fear the plumbing will show. Manufacturers have long since answered that problem with solutions like this chrome trap cover. Wall-mount sinks can always be as sleek and hip as any other type, so if space constraints are a concern, you have an option.

WALL-MOUNT HIS-AND-HERS SINKS. Wall-mounted sinks can be your super-cool choice for space-saving his-and-her features in a master bath. This duo shows just how much style can be packed into a small footprint. Set against a posh tiled wall, the sinks present attractive curved forms and slick chrome trap covers that make sharp accents out of what could be staid eyesores.

Chic Wall-Mount Sinks

PICK A TROUGH SINK FOR EXTRA ROOM. Equip a busy bathroom with a useful and stylish fixture by mounting a trough sink. This sink is almost as easy to mount as a single-bowl unit and offers a lot more room to maneuver so that more than one person can use the sink at a time. It looks fantastic and adds a linear design element to the room. Trough sinks (and wall-mounted units in general) are well served by a standalone undersink shelf, such as the wood piece in this bathroom. It's a great way to introduce accessible storage space.

USE SINGLE-HANDLE FAUCETS ON WALL-MOUNTED SINKS. Make the most of the modest deck space on a wall-mounted sink by using a single-handled faucet. As these sinks show, deck space for soap, perfume, or other bathroom essentials is extremely limited. Single-handled faucets are streamlined and leave plenty of open space on the rest of the sink's deck. They are easy to install, and easier to operate for small children or people with disabilities.

EMBELLISH A WALL-MOUNT SINK WITH ACCENTS. Use small details to embellish the relatively simple form of most wall-mounted sinks. The curved front edge of this sink is complemented with a curving piece of metal below it, there for nothing more than a decorative flourish (and also serving as a hand-towel rack). The gooseneck faucet is a graceful accent playing off the other curving shapes.

MATCH SINK SHAPE TO OTHER FIXTURES. Look for guidance in choosing a sink by taking cues from the room's style. Here, a modern look and rectangular bathtub are perfectly partnered with a blocky wall-mounted sink. The shape means more space in the bowl then there would be with a round sink, and the lines of the sink—as well as the modern faucet—blend perfectly with the other decorative elements.

Chic Pedestal & Console Sinks

CONSOLE SINKS BRING PANACHE. Add simple elegance to a small bathroom with a sophisticated console sink. This style comes in both curving and square shapes, but both feature chrome legs with crossbars that can be used to hang towels. Add a bit of storage by buying a unit with a lower shelf, as this sink has. The glass shelf is a good way to incorporate a useful surface without weighing down the airy and elegant appearance a console sink brings to a room.

FINISHES HELP CONSOLES STAND OUT. Console sinks are minimal by nature, but that doesn't mean that you have to settle for the most common chrome support structure. The gold legs on these twin console sinks are just one example of alternative finishes to chrome. You can also find stainless steel, brushed nickel and bronze among other leg and crossbrace finishes. Choose the one that best accents your bathroom design.

REINTERPRET STANDARD SINK STYLES. Don't feel you have to stick to white porcelain and chrome just because you want the open and airy look of a console sink. This model is an example of a complete reinterpretation of the style. An iron base holds a hammered copper body with integral sink. It's a completely unique look, dark and dramatic. The unit includes a shelf underneath and lots of deck space for a soap dish and anything else you might want to put there. A matching faucet caps off a look that is rich in texture and wholly unexpected.

MODERN ROOMS INVITE INNOVATION. If modern style is your look of choice for a bathroom, consider a modern interpretation of the pedestal sink. This cylindrical sink offers a stunning design element for the right bathroom. All the plumbing is concealed. The form is alluring, and it works perfectly when combined with other modern elements, such as the floating shelves and floor-mounted faucet.

FLOWING FORMS MAKE PEDESTALS STAND OUT. Add a bit of flair to a contemporary bathroom with a curvy, sensuous pedestal shape. Pedestal sinks can be plain or ornate, but a shape such as this makes a vivid first impression and works perfectly with a detailed tile pattern, such as the black wall surface behind this sink. The sleek single-handled faucet is also well matched to the sink.

DIAL BACK SINK STYLE IN LIVELY DECOR. A plain pedestal sink is often best for a bathroom featuring other exceptionally dynamic elements. The reflective red walls in this room dominate the space and grab the attention. Unembellished features, including a simple toilet and uncomplicated pedestal sink, allow the surface treatment to shine while still providing handsome visual features.

CHOOSE STYLISH PEDESTALS FOR INCREASED APPEAL. Even pedestal sinks can have design flair. This period-style sink brings a flourish to this stunning bathroom, popping out against a background of cobalt tiles and sitting between a toilet and bidet styled for the same time period. Both the pedestal and bowl are highly designed and detailed, creating a visual appeal far beyond the simple form or function of the fixture.

Chic Vessel Sinks

CREATE A FOCAL POINT WITH UNUSUAL MATERIALS. Looking for a standout sink? Vessel sinks may be the perfect option for you, and they are available in an astounding selection of materials and forms. This example is one of the more unusual, crafted in a slightly irregular oval of green onyx with the appearance inside of an abalone shell. It's a distinctive style that works perfectly with the surrounding decorative elements.

METAL VESSELS CAN MAKE A DESIGN. Metal vessel sinks are becoming increasingly popular, and if you want to add unique textures and interesting finishes to your bathroom, you could do a lot worse than one of these incredibly interesting fixtures. This formed metal bowl carries a tempered copper finish, with distinct mottling that makes it different from any other sink. A material such as this is best matched to other raw materials in the room, such as the interwoven copper wall surface and stone vanity counter.

Chic Vessel Sinks

SIMPLE VESSEL SINKS ARE ALWAYS IN STYLE. Add a modern look to a shared bathroom with simple and square his-and-her sinks mounted on top of a wall-hung slab. Where the plumbing runs behind the vessel, such as with these generous sinks, the drain can be run through the slab so that it's not visible from the top. This discreet placement creates a sleek appearance made even sleeker with the addition of a stainless steel rod on the front of the slab—the perfect hand-towel rack. Although you'll sacrifice some storage with a design like this, the open area under the sink increases the sense of space in the room.

CHOOSE A NICKEL FINISH FOR A SOPHISTICATED LOOK. Put a contemporary spin on a metal vessel sink by choosing one with a nickel finish. The finish is different enough from chrome to set itself apart, and this hand-worked metal vessel brings textural variations that highlight the beautiful finish. Take the easy road and match a nickel-finish sink to a brushed-nickel faucet and handles, as seen in this bathroom.

Chic Vessel Sinks

MOUNT VESSELS WITH WIT. Use a vessel sink to craft a one-of-kind look full of personality. This box-shaped stone vessel sink has been mounted offset from blocks framed out from the wall and clad in different types of stone. Coupled with a long, skinny mirror, orb lighting, and a wall-mount faucet, the look is full of style and surprise. You can create an equally impressive scene by placing your vessel sink in an unusual relationship to the counter or support.

MOUNT GLASS ON GLASS. If vessel sinks have captured your imagination, you'll find clear glass vessel sinks almost magical in how they confuse the eye. Water in the sink seems to almost be floating in midair, and the illusion is made even stronger by mounting the sink on a glass vanity counter. The look isn't right for every bathroom, but it can be stunning in a modern or streamlined contemporary bathroom—especially when coupled with a support such as this dark wood pillar. A combination like this can even serve as the focal point of a powder room.

TROUGH VESSEL SINKS ARE UNCOMMON BUT UNIQUE. Use a trough vessel sink in place of his-and-her sinks for an unusual, but every bit as useful, look. This sink is made of tinted and polished volcanic rock, with a back-edge drain. A vessel sink in an unusual shape and material can be a design centerpiece in the bathroom. Just be careful in choosing colorful sinks, because overly bold or trendy colors can become dated rather quickly.

FLAT VESSELS SURPRISE AND DELIGHT THE EYE. When super-stylish elegance is your bathroom-design goal, consider a "plate" vessel sink. These sinks are nearly flat and defy the description of a sink, but work just as well as any other. You need to be careful when matching a faucet to such a shallow sink to avoid splashing (adjusting water pressure can also control this). For an even more impressive effect, turn to a material such as nickel-finish hammered metal, used here.

Chic Vessel Sinks

USE SQUARE SINKS FOR ROOMY BASINS. Choose a square vessel when you want a lot of room in the bowl of the sink and where the shape complements other linear elements in the room design. The large white porcelain sink in this room goes perfectly with the shape of the vanity structure.

WEDGE VESSEL SINKS IN CORNERS. Vessel sinks are great solutions in tight spots because of their open appeal. This bathroom features a hammered copper sink with a rough natural texture that works well with the stone surfaces and faux wood timber counter support in the space. The effect created is a natural look, warm, comfortable and informal. The sink is just one standout element among many.

STONE VESSEL SINKS IMPRESS. Consider a stone vessel sink to make a big impression in a smaller space such as a powder room. Material such as unpolished marble contributes a rich texture and feel to the room. Stone sinks are a little pricier than other types, and they may need to be sealed against water and stain infiltration, but the end result is spectacular.

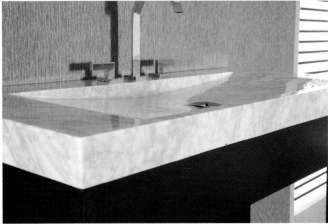

CONTEMPORARY CALLS FOR STREAMLINED SINKS. Stretch the definition of a vessel sink by using a countertop "tray" version such as this stone sink. This streamlined look is right at home in a contemporary bathroom. The basin is gently sloped for an unusual geometric appearance; the vanity counter is sized to perfectly complement the sink. It's a pleasing appearance that is easy to re-create regardless of the type of square or rectangular vessel sink you choose.

PLAY WITH VESSEL MOUNTING STYLE. Achieve interesting effects by using vessel sinks in unusual ways. Here, a clear glass vessel sink has been embedded in a floating glass countertop anchored to the wall by way of a wood frame. The chrome plumbing, fixtures and accents contribute to a clean, modern aesthetic, but the sink's relationship to the countertop is really the key visual in this area of the bathroom.

VITREOUS CHINA OFFERS A CLASSIC LOOK. Turn to vitreous china for an elegant and delicate vessel sink. The high-gloss finish and the fact that china sinks can be manufactured with relief designs such as the floral motif shown here make this option extremely attractive. These types of vessel sinks are most at home in more formal or traditional bathrooms.

Exceptional Hardware

Faucets and showerheads are the jewelry adorning the body of your bathroom design. They can be subtle and restrained, like background bit players in the drama of the design, or they can be front-and-center all stars. Usually, if the space is full of wonderful textures, patterns or incredible colors, it's best to choose hardware that is a bit restrained. When your design is rather placid—in an all-white bathroom, for instance—faucets and showerheads can be a bit flashier. Faucets, especially, are available in an amazing number of finishes and spout styles, for both sinks and tubs.

Of course, faucets and showerheads are first and foremost important functional aspects in the bathroom. Select a faucet that serves the size and shape of sink you've installed, with handles that work for the people who will use the bathroom the most.

The same goes for showerheads. Water conservation is a big issue across the country and may determine the type and number of showerheads you require. You'll also want a showerhead that provides you with the type of spray you prefer. An overhead rainwater showerhead is a gentle wake-me-up in the morning that many people find enjoyable. Others like a bracing blast of water from a high-power head sticking right out of the wall.

Settle on the fixtures that serve your needs and preferences best, and pick a specific style and finish that will embellish your bathroom's design.

GOOSENECK FAUCETS ADD ELEGANCE AND STYLE. Gooseneck faucets are some of the most popular because their graceful form embellishes the appearance of just about any sink. If you want a slightly more unique look in a gooseneck faucet, you might choose something like this one, with its faceted, geometric form. The faucet is well matched to the squared-off sink and is an interesting take on the traditional gooseneck form.

A SPECIAL SINK CALLS FOR A SPECIAL FAUCET. This concrete sink with edge drain is an over-the-top feature begging for a faucet as equally stunning. This three-hole modern version mightily answers the call. The crude, rough texture of the stone contrasts the super-smooth polished nickel surface of the faucet, and the faucet's clean, curving lines pop out against the rough, hard lines of the sink. It's a marriage of contrast, but one that works beautifully.

Divine Faucets

DARK FAUCETS WORK BEST WITH DARK FURNISHINGS. Antiqued faucet finishes continue to be popular, and it's a style that might work well in your bathroom—especially if your bathroom furniture is finished dark brown or ebony. This bathroom's taupe walls complement the color of the faucet, and accessories match to create a lovely unified design. Crisp white wainscoting ensures that the antiqued finishes and darker colors don't overwhelm the space.

MOUNT UNUSUAL FAUCETS ON SIMPLE SINKS. The accents you choose in a small bathroom have a lot of visual power. Even a small detail such as a faucet can affect the look of the room—especially a distinctive faucet such as this. The porcelain body forms a pitcher for the water, while the metal handle controls the flow. It's a wonderful combination and a truly interesting visual that livens up the bathroom.

EXTREME FAUCET STYLES SERVE DISTINCTIVE DECORS. Choose a highly evocative faucet to match your particular aesthetic when you're designing a bathroom in a distinctive style. This modern bathroom called for accents that reinforced the angular, linear nature of the room. The faucet—and the light fixture that complements it—plays right into the design style while being almost a work of art itself. An enlightened selection of accents such as faucets can make or break a bathroom's look and feel.

WATERFALL FAUCETS ADD WHIMSY. Looking for something different in your contemporary bathroom? Look no further. A waterfall faucet looks whimsical when it's running and sleek when it's not. This stunning accent can be a big part of the room's design but won't break the bank. Just make sure that you don't fall in love with the faucet to the exclusion of the sink! This is a distinctive contemporary style that isn't right for every sink or every bathroom. It calls for a simpler, linear sink to show it at its best.

USE CLASSIC FAUCETS WITH CLASSIC DECORATIVE ELEMENTS. The wisest move is often to match your faucet choice to your bathroom style. Although many wild faucet designs are made and sold, classic is best for a room like this, which features traditional wainscoting and a traditionally styled pedestal sink. The chrome finish complements the sink, and the elegant gooseneck form is ideal for this setting.

PICK A WALL-MOUNT FAUCET TO SUIT ROOM STYLE. Most wall-mounted faucets are crafted in a contemporary or modern style, but that's not a hard-and-fast rule. When you need a wall-mounted faucet for a more distinct style of sink, such as the antiqued hand-wrought finish of this undermount, or when your choice of vanity top has no holes, you can find one to match. This country-style faucet is a perfect example.

Divine Faucets

A FAUCET MUST COMPLEMENT THE SINK. Match your faucet to your sink for a visual that is much more than the sum of its parts. Choosing the perfect faucet is a decision born of both art and science, but take cues from your sink's shape and form and you'll rarely go wrong. The elegant L-bend faucet coupled with this vessel sink contains the same circular aspect in its tubular form as the sink does in its overall shape. The chrome finish goes perfectly with the white porcelain sink—a natural, classic marriage that you can replicate in your bathroom.

DISPLAY YOUR TASTES WITH A UNIQUE FAUCET FINISH. Tap the amazing number of bathroom sink faucet finishes for one that personalizes the look of your bathroom. This faucet boasts an unusual gold finish that matches the handles and hinges on the vanity. Gold is an unexpected touch in the bathroom, and when used against a larger, neutral background, it can really make for an appealing look.

ASYMMETRICAL WALL-MOUNTS WORK. Enhance your contemporary or modern bathroom with a non-centered wall-mount faucet. These elements eliminate the appearance of plumbing pipes under a wall-mount vanity or sink and streamline the look of fixtures. Some wall-mount faucets simply jut out from the wall with a modest mounting ring; this alternative features a sharp mounting plate for a clean and sophisticated appearance. If you're looking for a slick accent that really drives home a modern aesthetic, you could do a lot worse than installing an offset wall-mount faucet.

LEVER HANDLES ARE EASY TO USE. Choose lever handles for any faucet that will be used by young children, the elderly or people with disabilities. Levers are much easier to operate than conventional twist handles, and they also look great. The styling of levers can be elegantly lyrical or sometimes as stunning as the faucet shape itself. Just be sure that the levers you choose will clear any lip of a top-mount or vessel sink.

Superior Showerheads

THE FIXTURES MAKE THE SHOWER. Add special shower fixtures to turn even a modest shower stall into a luxurious enclosure. Fixtures such as the body-side spray nozzles lining the tiled walls of this shower create a full-body shower experience. This shower also includes a stunning rainwater showerhead and a handheld showerhead connected to an adjustable bar. All the different spray points make it possible to adjust the shower for any particular desired strength, direction or combination of sprays.

SLIDE-BARS INCREASE USABILITY. Make your shower extremely adaptable by adding a sliding bar-mount showerhead. The showerhead can be adjusted to any height up or down the pole and angled as the user wishes—creating a fixed spray exactly where the bather wants it. The showerhead can also be removed from its bracket and used as a handheld shower wand. Newer versions, like this flat paddle head, are not only more chic than their predecessors, they also offer a more luxurious spray.

USE SQUARE FIXTURES WHERE ROUND IS EXPECTED. Introduce a cool accent to a contemporary shower enclosure by using a showerhead and hardware in unexpected shapes. The "cube" fixtures here are visually interesting and surprising, reinterpreting the traditional round shape of a showerhead and controls. The shape of these elements complements the shape of the shower enclosure itself, as well as the frameless glass wall.

UNCONVENTIONAL FIXTURES ADD LUXURY AND STYLE. Don't be trapped by convention when selecting showerheads and spray fixtures. Although wall nozzles and overhead rainwater showerheads are more common, go with a more unique look by choosing wall spray tiles and a blocky head. These spray fixtures, including the head, are all adjustable and can be set to different types of spray patterns. The look is slick, chic and extraordinary—just right for a distinctive bath with slate-tiled walls and wood accents.

Superior Showerheads

TOWERS ENRICH SHOWERS. Complete shower consoles (also known as "towers") are impressive additions to even a modest shower enclosure. The look is sleek and modern and well suited to a chic surface, such as this surround covered in mosaic glass tiles. The console routes water to the showerhead and serves as the central control tower for the shower, including an array of spray heads that can be opened or closed to suit the individual. It's a luxurious shower experience no matter how you look at it.

USE SIMPLE SHOWERHEADS ON SIMPLE SURFACES. Despite the temptingly sophisticated and complex showerhead systems with additional features like steam heads, it is often the case that a simple solution works as well or better. This basic, single-handle showerhead looks just right against a backdrop of old-world stone tile. It was also easy to install because the plumbing from the handle to the head is piped outside the wall, rather than being plumbed inside it. The large showerhead still provides a refreshing shower experience and looks great while doing so.

LUXURIATE WITH MULTIPLE SHOWERHEADS. Several showerheads spraying in multiple directions provide one of the most invigorating showers you'll ever experience. The key is adjustability. The shower sprayers on the side wall in this enclosure can be turned off, as can the hand sprayer. You can completely control how much or little spray the shower provides. Notice the antique styling of the heads in this shower; they blend perfectly with the mottled wall surfacing.

Superior Showerheads

HANDHELD SHOWERHEADS ARE ALWAYS HANDY. Slide-bar showerheads are some of the most useful, because the spray can be adjusted to any height along the bar. Most slide-bar sets come equipped with a handheld showerhead that is usually secured in a bracket, as it is here. But the head can be removed, making the hardware even more useful. There's no denying that the bar adds an attractive vertical element within the shower enclosure.

PLUMB FOR THE FEATURES YOU WANT. An overhead rainwater showerhead provides a luxurious experience few people can resist. But running plumbing overhead can be a daunting project. Avoid the challenge of plumbing inside a wall and a ceiling by using a fixture such as the one shown in this shower. The overhead showerhead is plumbed to the handle through an exterior pipe, all styled to look cool and hip. A handheld wand showerhead complements the fixture and completes the sumptuous shower.

Fantastic Tub Faucets

TUB FAUCETS ARE DESIGN OPPORTUNITIES. Open up your design with a freestanding bathtub, but don't forget the design power the right freestanding faucet can bring. As this fixture shows, hardware servicing freestanding tubs that don't abut a wall can be beautiful to the point of poetry. This faucet assembly features an elegant gooseneck spout and a separate handheld head for washing the shampoo out of your hair. As useful as it is, this is just as much a design accent that improves the look of the room.

ENSURE SUCCESS BY MATCHING THE FAUCET FINISH TO THE TUB. If your tub has a unique finish, such as the brushed nickel of this pedestal tub, you can play it safe by using a faucet in a matching finish, allowing the tub's appearance to take center stage. This faucet doesn't give up any style points with its elegant gooseneck spout and hand-held wand attachment. It's an ideal pairing between hardware and tub.

HANDHELD MOUNTS CAN EMBELLISH ENTIRE WALLS. Most handheld wands are hung off the faucet body itself, but the look here is even sharper with the wand having its own wall mount. This keeps the wand up and out of the way of the faucet controls and looks great. Notice that the chrome faucet, wand and hose are perfectly compatible with the sleek look of the pedestal tub.

MINIMAL TUB FAUCETS FIT MOST TUB STYLES. Turn to modern and minimal faucet styles for a floor-mount faucet that suits many different bathroom and bathtub styles. This casual and informal bathroom includes a tub with an old-time rolled lip and hanging kettle bells, but the elegant and spare gooseneck faucet—supported on a small circular foot—blends right in without making much noise. It's a lovely accent that doesn't overpower or confuse the look of the room.

EMBELLISH DISTINCTIVE TUBS WITH STYLED FAUCETS. A country-style deck-mounted tub is well served by an impressive faucet with a telephone-style cradle for the handheld sprayer attachment. A clean, chrome finish is a natural choice for a homey, white room such as this, and the ornate style of the faucet really shines against the plainer background of white wainscoting and matching tub surround. The faucet is also perfectly placed to be handy for anyone taking a bath.

PLAY WITH BATHTUB FAUCET PLACEMENT. Don't be a slave to convention when choosing where to place your bathtub faucet. Depending on the type of tub you have and where it's located in the bathroom, there may be several different potential locations for the faucet. Positioning such as this, with the faucet on one side and the controls on the other, creates a balanced and interesting look. It also moves the faucet away from the ends of the tub, where a bather's head is most likely to rest.

The Well-Lit Bathroom

The right lighting is crucial for keeping a bathroom safe and putting the best face on the room's design. The best bathroom lighting accommodates different users and many different situations. It must ensure against trips or falls as bathers get in and out of a tub and make any face in the vanity mirror look as close to what will be seen in daylight as possible. The fixtures themselves should look good or at least be subtle enough not to affect the design in a negative way.

Achieving all those goals usually requires different types of lighting throughout a bathroom. A general ambient light source is essential for any bathroom, from a powder room to a large, luxurious master bathroom. Most bathrooms will also need the proper mirror lighting, as well as specific lighting for areas such as a standalone shower enclosure.

Various types of lighting combine to show off your decorative elements without annoying shadows or hot spots. Certain fixtures can also become decorative elements, especially those used around the mirror. You can find fixtures in any type of style, from country farmhouse to modern. Whichever you choose, always make sure the illumination they supply is all the light the room needs to shine.

BALANCED LIGHTING PUTS YOUR BEST FACE FORWARD. Long vanities with undivided mirrors on the wall require creative lighting to make the image in the mirror as true to life as possible. Here, strong side lights are used to project light across the mirror, but highlights positioned over the vanity offer fill lighting. When coordinating two or more sets of lights like this, put the lights on a dimmer switch whenever possible. That will let you adjust until you get the level of illumination that works best for you.

LIGHT DUAL MIRRORS EVENLY. The most common placement for vanity lights is on either side of the mirror. This particular bathroom matches his-and-her mirrors to the twin sinks below, creating a very symmetrical look. The best way to light dual mirrors is to use three fixtures so that each mirror is lit from both sides. These fixtures are fitted with elegant shades that look lovely but, more importantly, prevent any hot spots in the field of view and create a nice, diffused light.

MINIMIZE LIGHT REFLECTION WITH MUTED TOP LIGHTS. Where it's impractical to install lights along the sides of a vanity mirror, you still need to use lights specifically for the mirror area. Many times, this involves adding a strip of lights over the top of the mirror. These lights were carefully positioned high enough so there are no bright spot reflections for anyone looking in the mirror. The plastic shades diffuse the light, which helps avoid dark facial shadows that occur when strong light is directed down the mirror.

CONTROL BATHROOM LIGHTING. Put strong vanity lights—and all lights in the bathroom, if you can—on a dimmer switch. The bright lights on either side of this framed vanity mirror leave the image in the mirror crystal clear, but they sometimes may be too bright for users' comfort. In those instances, dim the lights to create a lovely mood or simply to suit an individual's preference.

Marvelous Vanity Lights

MOUNT LIGHTS THROUGH THE MIRROR. Incorporate a cool, contemporary accent into your modern bathroom design by mounting vanity side lights right through a wide mirror. Although you'll need some help from a glass fabricator or mirror professional, the look is interesting and original and can also be a way to include side lights when there isn't any room alongside the mirror.

PICK LIGHT SHADES FOR GOOD SKIN TONES. When using over-mirror lights such as these three fixtures, it's wise to outfit them with low-wattage, soft white bulbs. The softer light, especially diffused through a skin-flattering yellow lampshade, shows skin tones more accurately and with fewer harsh shadows. Bright is good for close personal grooming, but a softer, milder light works really well for checking your image as others see it.

TUBE LIGHTS SERVE MOST BATHROOMS WELL. You can use over-mirror tube lights for dispersed illumination, easy installation, and a simple, streamlined look. The appearance of the fixture fits especially well in a contemporary bathroom such as this one. If you decide to choose this type of vanity light, it's wise to use one that runs the entire width of the mirror for maximum light spread.

RECESSED LIGHTS WORK EVERYWHERE. Recessed ceiling lights are effective general lighting solutions, especially for an area such as the open shower shown here. Not only do the lights ensure safety in the shower and adjacent areas, but the bright halogen lights also make the stunning glass-tiled surfaces of this shower sparkle. Dress up any shower enclosure by completely tiling all the surfaces. Keep in mind that any lighting fixture used in a shower enclosure needs to be sealed against the moisture.

DIRECT LIGHTING WITH TRACK HEADS. Use track lighting as an adjustable source of ambient light in a large bathroom. You can purchase subtle tracks and lighting heads that blend into the design and use them where direct lighting is needed most (here, they not only create a safer environment around the tub, they also fill in the shadows left by the sconce uplights on either side of the mirror). Track lights are especially effective in a room such as this, where abundant reflective surfaces bounce and amplify the light, ensuring excellent full-room illumination.

Ideal General Lighting

USE RECESSED CEILING LIGHTS WHEREVER YOU NEED BRIGHT, CLEAR, GENERAL LIGHT. Use recessed ceiling lights wherever you need bright, clear general light. The recessed fixtures broadcast light evenly down from the ceiling and are an understated look suitable for many different styles of bathroom. Although they take some work to install, they can be added almost anywhere you need bright light for safety or personal grooming. The best recessed fixtures include adjustable heads, allowing you to change the direction of the light and customize the room's lighting to suit your needs or mood.

LIGHT FOR SAFETY. A single light such as this can work perfectly for ensuring safety around a tub or shower. The light can be put on a separate switch or added to an existing circuit. The light may not seem overpowering, but it only needs to give the eye a clear idea of where water has splashed and where the floor and tub deck are dry.

LIGHT-AND-FAN COMBOS ARE DOUBLY USEFUL. A general overhead light fixture can serve a smaller bathroom all by itself and provide much of the light needed in a larger space. This fixture is unique in that it incorporates a vent fan into the base. Combination fan-light fixtures are useful in any bathroom that has ductwork in place for the vent.

LOW-KEY LIGHT FIXTURES SUPPORT A STRONG DESIGN. Keep your overhead lighting fixture understated if you want other elements in the bathroom's design to grab the attention. A stunning neo-round shower enclosure with dynamic tilework is meant to take center stage in this bathroom. The large wall-mounted sink is a secondary player, but the lighting fixtures, including the bright central fixture, are merely meant to support the other stars of the design.

Bathroom Extras

Even though the functions of a bathroom are fairly basic, there are actually quite a few elements you can introduce into your bathroom to make it more accessible, comfortable, usable and beautiful.

All of these extra features have some sort impact—small or large—on the room's design. Modest additions such as vanity-top accents, hanging towel hooks and shaving mirrors are easy to include because they don't cost much and take relatively little work to install.

More significant bathroom extras may entail a big investment in time, money or both. Big changes to make a bathroom accessible for the elderly or the disabled are often matters of necessity, but that doesn't mean they have to look less than attractive. You can equip your bathroom with these Universal Design features and still have a good-looking space.

Of course, you can also opt to add pure luxury features like a sauna or skylight. These change the whole character of the room in profound ways. Many, such as well-appointed makeup areas, have the potential to impact your day-to-day life as well. The larger the addition, the more you need to weigh the pros and cons.

Choose from among the many options that follow based on the size of your bathroom and your budget and on exactly how you want to use the altered room. And, of course, always weigh how the feature affects the bathroom's design.

STYLIZE SPECIAL-NEEDS FEATURES. Don't give up on good design simply because you have to set up the room for users with special needs. This neat, trim and spare roll-in shower is an example of Universal Design integrated in a visually pleasing minimalist aesthetic. The sink is also adapted to suit a wheelchair-bound user but still looks handsome enough for any bathroom. As an added bonus, both features make the bathroom easier to use whether you have special needs or not.

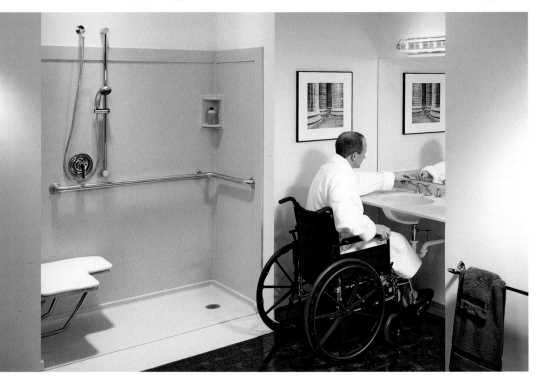

Attractive Universal Design

BLEND SAFETY FEATURES INTO THE DESIGN. The Universal Design elements in this bathroom are so well integrated into the look that they hardly seem like something extra at all. Grab bars for the shower, bath and toilet are all positioned according to established guidelines, but the brushed nickel finish really blends these features. The finish is easy on the eyes and matches the faucet and toilet paper holder. There's no reason that the accessibility features you add to your bathroom can't look this good.

PICK A TUB THAT HELPS THE BATHER. Special-access tubs with swing-in doors are your best friend when designing a bathroom to accommodate users with limited mobility. These tubs are built with special seating that is easy to get in and out of and a door that seals perfectly to prevent water from leaking out. The tubs are perfect for the elderly or people with mobility problems, and the small footprint ensures that they can easily fit into most bathroom floor plans.

Attractive Universal Design

GRAB BARS ARE DESIGN ACCENTS. Make your Universal Design bathroom as attractive as possible by blending accessibility elements into the design at large. A common high-quality tiled wall makes this roll-in shower stall look absolutely natural, like an intentional part of the room's decor. Chrome grab bars positioned strategically throughout the room complement the chrome on the roll-under sink, which is itself elegantly styled to look like a design high point. Every element of the room's design exhibits a thoughtfulness and aesthetic savvy that improves use while improving the look of the space.

ERGONOMIC FIXTURES AID BATHROOM ACCESSIBILITY. Add specially designed fixtures in a bathroom used by people with disabilities or coordination and mobility issues. This ergonomic shower sprayer is mounted on a grab bar and has special grips built in to ensure that it can be held securely by someone with poor hand strength or other problems.

POSITION GRAB BARS FOR MAXIMUM EFFICIENCY. Designing a bathroom that adheres to the standards of Universal Design means adding specific specialized features in just the right places. Don't assume that you can use any grab bar for any application; this special crooked bar is specifically meant as an aid to use a toilet, and its position on the wall is well thought out to provide all the leverage a person with limited mobility needs to get up and down.

Handy Makeup Areas

EXPLOIT BATHROOM CORNERS. You can often find space for a makeup area in the corner of a bathroom. Corners tend to be dead areas in these rooms, and a small corner table like this one can be positioned between vanities and sinks. You'll find many prefabricated corner cabinets, desks and counters to suit this type of installation, or you can create your own custom installation for a standalone makeup area.

MAKEUP FITS IN MODEST SPACES. You don't necessarily need a lot of room for a well-appointed makeup area. This wonderful small desk addition to the side of a detailed vanity provides all the space necessary for the lady of the house to paint her nails or apply lipstick and makeup. The cushioned upholstered chair is a great addition and an ideal element in any makeup area.

MATCH MAKEUP TABLES TO OTHER FURNITURE. The key to adding a makeup area in your bathroom without disrupting the design is to blend the elements that define the area with the other furniture and fixtures in the room. This small makeup desk is crafted of the same wood as the connected vanity and the built-in storage units on each side. This creates a pleasingly unified look so that each area of the room runs seamlessly into the next.

Handy Makeup Areas

A FULL-SIZE MIRROR ADDS TO A MAKEUP AREA. Most makeup areas in a bathroom include a small mirror as an essential feature for using the area to its best advantage. However, there's no reason why you can't include a full-size mirror to make the area even more useful. The makeup desk in this bathroom includes a mirror identical to what is used for the vanity, with sidelights and frame that create design continuity.

Super Saunas

BUY A SAUNA KIT FOR YOUR CORNER. Do you have a lot of extra room in your bathroom and want to add a big luxury feature? A sauna is a healthy retreat from the day's stress and comfortably fits in the corner of a larger bathroom. Saunas such as this are often sold as complete kits—just be sure you measure carefully to ensure the finished structure fits properly into the available space.

CORNER SAUNAS FIT TIGHT SPOTS. Put extra floor space to use in a larger bathroom with a corner sauna. A unit such as this is an incredible luxury in a bathroom, and even though it can fit up to four people, the corner orientation ensures that the sauna takes up as little floor space as possible. Placing it next to a tub or shower only makes sense because the two experiences go hand in hand.

Super Saunas

TINY SAUNAS WORK IN SMALLER ROOMS. Incorporate affordable luxury into a large bathroom with a one- or two-person sauna. Smaller and more compact than most units, these can usually fit in a corner or next to a shower enclosure. Many prefab saunas are entirely self-contained—all they need is an electrical outlet. As this one clearly shows, prefabricated units don't sacrifice style to function—they look as nice as they work.

CONVERT A CLOSET TO A SAUNA. You may think you don't have the room for a fabulous sauna, but sometimes it's just a matter of looking in the right place. An unused closet next to this bathroom has been converted to a small but serviceable sauna. An integral vent fan and modest heating stove serve the small space well, adding a big touch of luxury to a small room.

ADD LIGHT AND AIR FROM ABOVE. Add a roof window over a shower that needs both light and venting. A roof window is an operable skylight that provides a chance to air out a steamy room while allowing for tons of daylight. Roof windows like this are not terribly hard to install as long as the bathroom is located right underneath the roof rather than under another room.

FLARED SHAFTS SPREAD LIGHT. Where your bathroom is limited to modest clerestory windows, you can find much-needed natural light by adding a large skylight. The skylight in this room is not only sizable, but it has also been installed in a flared shaft, ensuring the light penetrates throughout the bathroom. Retrofitting your bathroom with a big skylight involves a lot of expense and work, but the stunning benefits are pretty obvious—and obviously pretty.

TUNNEL SKYLIGHTS OFFER UNEXPECTED ILLUMINATION. Use tunnel skylights to illuminate a bathroom with specific spots of daylight. These unique fixtures are literally tunnels routed from a lens in the roof, down through a reflective tube, to the lens in the ceiling of the bathroom. Because of the way the ceiling lens is manufactured and installed, it disperses the light and brightens the room far more than its small size indicates.

TUNNEL SKYLIGHT BEFORE-AND-AFTER. Brighten any bathroom far beyond what you might anticipate with the addition of tunnel skylights. See the difference between a room lit by artificial fixtures (left) and the same room equipped with a tunnel skylight (right). The difference is astounding.

LIGHT A DARK, SMALL ROOM WITH A TUNNEL. One of the best features about a tunnel skylight is that it can reach into rooms that can't be fitted with a traditional skylight. Because the tunnel is flexible, it can be routed around structural members from the roof to the bathroom's ceiling. This powder room is far below the ceiling, and installing a skylight entails significant structural alterations—an expense that simply doesn't make sense for such a small room. But a tunnel light is a much more modest expense and one that still floods the small room with natural light throughout the day.

INCREASE SPACE WITH A SKYLIGHT. Skylights are a way for you to visually open up a small or odd-shaped bathroom, making it appear more airy and spacious. That's what has been done in this room, where two skylights overhead open the room to the skies. Because of the skinny shape of the room and the cant of the ceiling, the view out of the skylights is reflected in the vanity mirror, making the design even more intriguing.

SKYLIGHTS BRIGHTEN DARK ROOMS. Skylights or roof windows can be incredibly powerful elements in a room where dark materials cover much of the surface area. The dark stone tile in this luxury bath might have closed in the look of the room if not for soaring ceilings and two well-placed roof windows. The windows bring abundant light but also provide a starry view of the night sky when the homeowner is relaxing in the bath at twilight. The fact that they open means they also offer fresh air when needed.

Stunning Skylights & Windows

SOAK A BATHTUB WITH NATURAL LIGHT FROM ABOVE. Make an attic or top-floor bathroom a stunning sun-washed space by adding basic skylights. The impact of even simple flat skylights is incredibly powerful. At night, these units read black, and artificial light creates a different atmosphere in the room. During the day, the room needs no help to be perfectly illuminated.

UNUSUAL WINDOWS BRING LIGHT AND DRAMA. Add detailed windows to your bathroom to not only take advantage of a great view but to also to frame a hallmark tub. Windows such as these fixed divided panes add immensely to the bathroom design, but the real draw is the incredible view. This type of treatment works best when a year-round view is available, unencumbered by structures that might have people looking back in at you.

GLASS BLOCK COMBINES LIGHT AND PRIVACY. Although glass block is not as popular as it once was, it remains an excellent material for a bathroom window. Light, inexpensive and easy to work with, glass block achieves the two aims of any bathroom window: it lets the maximum amount of light into the room while maintaining the maximum amount of privacy. Glass block comes in many different surface textures, including abstract designs and more regular machined textures. You can even choose colored glass block.

WINDOW WALLS DRIVE DESIGN. Where an opulent spa-like tub setting abuts a wall, a full-wall window can complete the scene. This is especially true when the room has a soaring cathedral ceiling. This wall of glass opens the room and offers a stunning panorama night or day. Half-height window shades provide privacy as needed and are an excellent window treatment for any bathroom.

Towel Warmers

HARDWIRE A TOWEL WARMER FOR AN AFFORDABLE INDULGENCE. Bring a big touch of luxury to your modest guest bath with a wall-mounted, hardwired towel warmer. A rack such as this can hold many different towels for drying or warming fresh towels, and the chrome finish fits with most bathroom design styles. You can also find white or black versions if that's a better look for your bathroom; choose a plug-in version where you'd prefer not to wire in the unit.

PICK A TOWEL WARMER TO FIT AVAILABLE SPACE. When you don't have the room or inclination to add a wall-mounted or freestanding towel warmer rack, it doesn't mean the luxury is lost; a towel-warmer drawer can be easily built into a column of shelves or a linen closet and will keep your towels toasty for extravagant bathing.

LARGE TOWEL WARMERS SERVE BUSY ROOMS. Install a full-length towel warmer for all the towel storage you need—including space for both fresh and wet towels. A towel warmer such as the one in this pristine white bathroom can dry and warm towels quickly, and it also adds an interesting ladder-like visual. Wired-in warmers take a little more effort and expense, but the convenience of a warm towel at the flip of a switch is usually well worth the investment.

USE TOWEL WARMERS AS BACKGROUND ACCENTS. Choose a towel warmer rack that suits the available space, as well as the style of your bathroom. Here, leopard-print vessel sinks grab most of the attention, and the towel warmer is merely meant to fit in—a role for which the highly adaptable chrome finish is perfectly suited. But the space in this bathroom was constricted, leaving no wall area large enough for a standard-size towel warmer. This narrower version does the job just as well, though, and fits perfectly in a postage-stamp-sized location on the wall.

Mirror Style

A TILTING MIRROR ADDS FUNCTION AND FORM. If you decide to use a mirror without a medicine chest, your options are wide open. This oval mirror is attached to pivot mounts, which allow it to be tilted to suit the height of the viewer. A smaller, wall-mounted personal mirror serves personal grooming chores such as shaving or applying lipstick. The combination of mirrors ensures that this bathroom is as useful as it is attractive.

SIMPLE MIRRORS FOR SLEEK SPACES. A wide frameless mirror such as this is a chic look for a modern or contemporary bathroom. The wider perspective opens up the room, making it feel lighter and more spacious. The frameless style is perfect coupled with vessel sinks and trendy lights like the white, over-mirror fixtures.

ROUND MIRRORS ARE WHIMSICAL. Round mirrors are informal and capture a sense of fun in the bathroom. As this bathroom shows, a round mirror is perfect for funky bathroom style that includes unusual pendant lights on each side of the mirror, a metal vessel sink and mod wall-mount faucet. The frosted-glass mirror frame complements all the other eclectic elements.

MATCH MIRROR FRAMES TO DISTINCTIVE SURFACES. Use a mirror frame as the opportunity to accent the room's design and reinforce the style set by the sink and vanity. Here, a rustic wood vanity with copper undermount sink creates a definitive look. The hammered copper mirror frame perfectly complements the look and adds interest around the mirror.

FLUSH-MOUNT MIRRORS ARE CLEAN AND MODERN. Use a flush-mount medicine chest to recess a vanity mirror for a sleek aesthetic in the most modern of bathrooms. A chest and mirror like the one shown here is a very simple installation, and the mirror is easy to keep clean. The mirror opens by touch, but otherwise it appears to be part of the wall. This is an especially effective technique in rooms with stunning shiny reflective tiled surfaces that seem super smooth.

ECHO DESIGN IN YOUR CHOICE OF MIRRORS. Your mirror should reflect some of the overriding design cues in the room. This bathroom features a lovely symmetry established with two pedestal sinks, matching soap dishes, and twin shelves over the sinks. It would have been unusual to use a single long mirror over both sinks. The square mirrors are also fairly formal, keeping with the formal chair rail and footed tub. Silver frames provide a nice accent that works with the color in the room.

TILE A MIRROR INTO A WALL. Blend your mirror into the surroundings—if not the architecture itself—by tiling it into the wall. The myriad tiles on the wall of this bathroom have been laid around the mirror; the edge tiles form a frame around the mirror itself. It's a seamless design choice, and the mirror seems contiguous with the tiled surface.

Exceptional Accents

IN THEMATIC ROOMS, USE CONSISTENT FIXTURES.
A stunning bathroom like this, with raw plywood walls, a chic sliding door concealing the bath compartment and the feel of a spa, requires subtle but elegant accents to complete the picture. Matching towel ring, brush hook and towel bars complement the ornate shelf supports and brushed nickel, antique-style faucets. A woven tray full of soaps in the form of river rocks is the icing on the cake as far as the accents go.

MATCH COUNTERTOP ACCESSORIES TO THE FIXTURES. You don't need to go wild with the accents in a bathroom to ensure that they make a big impact. This copper soap tray is made from the same material as the sink but incorporates a finely wrought design around the border. A plain glass vase with fresh-cut flowers looks great, as it would in any bathroom.

HOOKS ARE ALWAYS USEFUL DECORATIVE FEATURES. Add storage and flair to the bathroom with hooks mounted on the walls. Although they are small design additions, they come in a vast variety of styles, finishes and looks. They are also incredibly handy because hooks can be placed just about anywhere they are needed (including on tiled surfaces). You can add the exact number that suits your purposes; plus they're adaptable—a sturdy, stylish hook such as this can be used to hang towels, a bathrobe or a suit in preparation for dressing. Hanging it with a witty reference to pegboard surfaces behind it is a wonderful added touch.

Exceptional Accents

EVEN HANDLES PRESENT DESIGN OPPORTUNITIES. Accessorize your bathroom with door and drawer handles that say "special" in subtle ways. You would expect to find crystal handles like these on a dresser or nightstand. Added to vanity doors, the handles delight the eye and add points of sparkle in the bathroom— an outsized effect for such a small decorative feature. Handles are the perfect decorative feature with which to experiment in the bathroom because they are inexpensive and so easy to change.

MATCH ACCENT FINISHES TO FAUCETS AND FIXTURES. Antique finishes have become more and more popular for the bathroom, not only for faucets but also for matching accents as well. This towel and hook combo shows the fine detailing available in accents, with slight distressing of the finish that makes the pieces look authentically antique. You'll find these types of accents available in copper tones, nickel and stainless steel surfaces, and even brass and gold.

ACCESSORIZE DRAWER PULLS, KNOBS OR OTHER BATHROOM HANDLES OR SPOUTS. Special drawer pulls are your way of adding a bit of flash to an otherwise visually sedate or subtle cabinet or vanity. Special design features, such as the tiny row of crystals in the center of these pulls, are ideal because the audience in a bathroom is often captive due to the functions of the room. Unexpected design flashes are a real treat to the eye and have outsized visual power in the limited space of a bathroom.

Resources

American Institute of Architects (AIA)
Their website includes information on Universal Design principles and resources and a list of members who practice Universal Design architecture.
www.aia.org
(202) 626-7300

American Association of Retired Persons (AARP)
Provides articles and information on Universal Design to accommodate elderly and disabled living.
www.aarp.org
(888) OUR-AARP

American Society of Interior Designers (ASID)
The society provides consumers with information about bathroom design, Universal Design practice and implementation in the design and a list of designers.
www.asid.org

(202) 546-3480

The Energy & Environmental Building Alliance (EEBA)
This organization offers networking and educational resources in promotion of sustainable building practices.
www.eeba.org
(952) 881-1098

National Association of the Remodeling Industry (NARI)
Offers comprehensive information on budgeting, planning and executing home remodeling projects, including bathroom redesigns, additions and remodels. The website provides listings of member contractors of all types.
www.nari.org
(847) 298-9200

National Kitchen & Bath Association (NKBA)
The NKBA inspires homeowners with a gallery of stunning bathroom designs, helps you plan and design your own bathroom remodel and

provides contact information for professionals that can help you bring it all together.
www.nkba.org
(800) 843-6522

United States Environmental Protection Agency—
Indoor Air Quality
In-depth information about materials and practices—including bathroom design concerns such as mold—that affect indoor air quality in homes nationwide.
www.epa.gov

United States Green Building Council
A non-profit dedicated to educating and helping consumers remodel, design, build and live in more environmentally friendly homes.
www.usgbc.org
(800) 795-1747

Photo Credits

Pages 38-39, all: Creative Publishing international

Page 40 top: Photo courtesy of Ceramic Tiles of Italy, www.italiatiles.com

Page 40 bottom: Photo courtesy of BR-111, www.br111.com, (800) 525-2711

Page 41: Photo courtesy of Crossville, Inc., www.crossvilleinc.com, (931) 484-2110

Page 42 top left: Photo courtesy of Oceanside Glasstile™, www.glasstile.com, (760) 929-5882

Page 42 top right: Photo courtesy of Ikea Home Furnishings, www.ikea-USA.com, (610) 834-0180

Page 42 bottom: Photo courtesy of Armstrong World Industries, www.armstrong.com, (717) 397-0611

Page 43 top: Photo courtesy of Hakatai Enterprises, www.hakatai.com, (888) 667-2429

Page 43 bottom left: Felix-Andrei Constantinescu / www.Shutterstock.com

Page 43 bottom right: Photo courtesy of Hakatai Enterprises, www.hakatai.com, (888) 667-2429

Page 44 top: Photo courtesy of Victoria + Albert, www.vandabaths.com

Page 44 bottom left: Photo courtesy of Van Robaeys/Inside/www.Beateworks.com

Page 44 bottom right: Photo courtesy of Jacuzzi, www.jacuzzi.com, (909) 606-1416

Page 45 top: Photo by Henrik Winther Andersen / www.Shutterstock.com

Page 45 bottom: Photo courtesy of Lacava, www.lacava.com, (888) 522-2823

Page 46: Photo by Baloncici / www.Shutterstock.com

Page 47 top: Photo courtesy of Merillat® Cabinetry, www.merillat.com

Page 47 bottom: Photo courtesy of Hakatai Enterprises, www.hakatai.com, (888) 667-2429

Page 48 top: Photo courtesy of Pyrolave USA, www.pyrolave.com

Page 48 bottom: Photo courtesy of Native Trails, Inc., www.nativetrails.net, (800) 786-0862

Page 49: Photo courtesy of ThinkGlass, www.thinkglass.com, (877) 410-4527

Page 50 top: Photo by aaphotograph / www.Shutterstock.com

Page 50 bottom: Photo by Justin Krug / www.Shutterstock.com

Page 51 top: Photo by Elena Elisseeva / www.Shutterstock.com

Page 51 bottom: Photo by Ioana Davies (Drutu) / www.Shutterstock.com

Page 52: Photo by Magdalena Bujak / www.Shutterstock.com

Page 53 top: Photo by Norman Pogson / www.Shutterstock.com

Page 53 bottom: Photo by photosphobos / www.Shutterstock.com

Page 54: Photo courtesy of Lacava, www.lacava.com, (888) 522-2823

Page 55: Photo courtesy of American Standard Brands, www.americanstandard-us.com, (800) 442-1902

Page 56 top left: Photo courtesy of Diamond Cabinets, www.diamond2.com

Page 56 top right: Photo courtesy of Madelli, Inc., www.madeli.com, (800) 819-6988

Page 56 bottom: Photo courtesy of Fairmont Designs, www.fairmontdesigns.com, (714) 670-1171

Page 57 top: Photo courtesy of Diamond Cabinets,m www.diamond2.com

Page 57 bottom left: Photo courtesy of Native Trails, Inc., www.nativetrails.net, (800) 786-0862

Page 57 bottom right: Photo courtesy of Native Trails, Inc., www.nativetrails.net, (800) 786-0862

Page 58: Photo by Francesco Grossi; design by Paolo Demarco, courtesy of Lacava, www.lacava.com, (888) 522-2823

Page 59 top left: Photo courtesy of Fairmont Designs, www.fairmontdesigns.com, (714) 670-1171

Page 59 top right: Photo courtesy of Madelli, Inc., www.madeli.com, (800) 819-6988

Page 59 bottom: Photo courtesy of Madelli, Inc., www.madeli.com, (800) 819-6988

Page 60 top left: Photo courtesy of Xylem Group, LLC, www.xylem.biz, (866) 395-8112

Page 60 top right: Photo courtesy of Xylem Group, LLC, www.xylem.biz, (866) 395-8112

Page 60 bottom: Tomasz Markowski / www.Shutterstock.com

Page 61: Photo courtesy of Fairmont Designs, www.fairmontdesigns.com, (714) 670-1171

Page 62 top: Photo courtesy of American Standard Brands, www.americanstandard-us.com, (800) 442-1902

Page 62 bottom left: Photo courtesy of Madelli, Inc., www.madeli.com, (800) 819-6988

Page 62 bottom right: Photo courtesy of Fairmont Designs, www.fairmontdesigns.com, (714) 670-1171

Page 63: Photo courtesy of The Furniture Guild, www.thefurnitureguild.com, (888) 479-4108

Page 64 top: Photo courtesy of Merillat® Cabinetry, www.merillat.com

Page 64 bottom: Photo by Michael Higginson / www.Shutterstock.com

Page 65 top left: Photo courtesy of Madelli, Inc., www.madeli.com, (800) 819-6988

Page 65 top right: Photo courtesy of Madelli, Inc., www.madeli.com, (800) 819-6988

Page 65 bottom: Creative Publishing international

Page 66: Photo courtesy of Lacava, www.lacava.com, (888) 522-2823

Page 67 top: Photo courtesy of Merillat® Cabinetry, www.merillat.com

Page 67 bottom: Photo by Breadmaker / www.Shutterstock.com

Page 68 top: Photo courtesy of Merillat® Cabinetry, www.merillat.com

Page 68 bottom: Photo by Tomasz Markowski / www.Shutterstock.com

Page 69 top: Photo courtesy of Moen, www.moen.com, (800) 289-6636

Page 69 bottom: Photo courtesy of Hansgrohe, www.hansgrohe-usa.com, (800) 334-0455

Page 70 top left: Photo by MAGENFX / www.Shutterstock.com

Page 70 top right: Photo by Eric Roth

Page 70 bottom: Istock

Page 71: Photo courtesy of Diamond Cabinets, www.diamond2.com

Page 72: Photo by Pics721 / www.Shutterstock.com

Page 73: Photo courtesy of BainUltra, Inc., www.bainultra.com, (800) 463-2187

Page 74 top: Photo courtesy of Sunrise Specialty Company, www.sunrisespecialty.com, (800) 444-4280

Page 74 bottom: Photo courtesy of Native Trails, Inc., www.nativetrails.net, (800) 786-0862

Page 75 top: Photo courtesy of Kohler, www.kohlerco.com, (800) 4 KOHLER

Page 75 bottom: Photo by Andrea Rugg for David Hiede Design

Page 76 top left: Photo courtesy of Victoria + Albert, www.vandabaths.com

Page 76 top right: Photo courtesy of BainUltra, Inc., www.bainultra.com, (800) 463-2187

Page 76 bottom: Photo by LuckyPhoto/ www.Shutterstock.com

Page 77: Photo by Marcos Sabugo, Photographer, www.marcossabugo.com, (561) 352-5585

Page 78 top: Photo by Melanie DeFazio / www.Shutterstock.com

Page 78 bottom: Photo courtesy of Native Trails, Inc., www.nativetrails.net, (800) 786-0862

Page 79 top: Photo courtesy of Sunrise Specialty Company, www.sunrisespecialty.com, (800) 444-4280

Page 79 bottom: Photo courtesy of Victoria + Albert, www.vandabaths.com

Page 80 top: Photo by Yampi / www.Shutterstock.com

Page 80 bottom: Photo courtesy of Kohler, www.kohlerco.com, (800) 4 KOHLER

Page 81: Istock/www.istock.com

Page 82 top: Photo by Haveseen / www.Shutterstock.com

Page 82 bottom: Photo courtesy of Jacuzzi, www.jacuzzi.com, (909) 606-1416

Page 83 top: Photo by Icyimage / www.Shutterstock.com

Page 83 bottom: Photo by Kostenko Maxim / www.Shutterstock.com

Page 84 top: Photo by Karen Melvin

Page 84 bottom: Photo by Ncn18 / www.Shutterstock.com

Page 85 top: Photo by Marin de Espinosa / www.Shutterstock.com

Page 85 bottom: Photo by Igor Borodin / www.Shutterstock.com

Page 86: Photo courtesy of Jacuzzi, www.jacuzzi.com, (909) 606-1416

Page 87 top: Photo courtesy of Diamond Spas, www.diamondspas.com

Page 87 bottom: Photo courtesy of MTI Whirlpools

Page 88 top: Photo by Sheldunov Andrew / www.Shutterstock.com

Page 88 bottom: Photo by Pics721 / www.Shutterstock.com

Page 89: Photo by aaphotograph / www.Shutterstock.com

Page 90 top: Photo courtesy of American Standard Brands, www.americanstandard-us.com, (800) 442-1902

Page 90 bottom: Photo by Phase4Photography / www.Shutterstock.com

Page 91: Photo by Anthony Berenyi / www.Shutterstock.com

Page 92: Photo by Paul Matthew Photography / www.Shutterstock.com

Page 93: Photo by Qiwen / www.Shutterstock.com

Page 94: Photo courtesy of Crossville, Inc., www.crossvilleinc.com, (931) 484-2110

Page 95 top: Photo courtesy of Hansgrohe, www.hansgrohe-usa.com, (800) 334-0455

Page 95 bottom: Photo courtesy of QuickDrain USA, www.quickdrainusa.com, (866) 998-6685

Page 96: Photo courtesy of American Standard Brands, www.americanstandard-us.com, (800) 442-1902

Page 97: Photo courtesy of Sunrise Specialty Company, www.sunrisespecialty.com, (800) 444-4280

Page 98 top right: Photo courtesy of Hakatai Enterprises, www.hakatai.com, (888) 667-2429

Page 98 left: Photo by Rade Kovac / www.Shutterstock.com

Page 98 bottom right: Photo courtesy of Hakatai Enterprises, www.hakatai.com, (888) 667-2429

Page 99 top: Photo by Gordana Sermek / www.Shutterstock.com

Page 99 bottom: Photo by Pics721 / www.Shutterstock.com

Page 100: Photo courtesy of Hakatai Enterprises, www.hakatai.com, (888) 667-2429

Page 101 top left: Photo by Mikeledray / www.Shutterstock.com

Page 101 bottom left: Photo by PhotoSky 4t com/ www.Shutterstock.com

Page 101 right: Photo by gh19 / www.Shutterstock.com

Page 102 left: Photo by Yampi / www.Shutterstock.com

Page 102 right: Photo by John Wollwerth / www.Shutterstock.com

Page 104: Photo by Kletr / www.Shutterstock.com

Page 105: Photo by Tr1sha / www.Shutterstock.com

Page 106 top: Photo by DCWCreations / www.Shutterstock.com

Page 106 bottom: Photo courtesy of American Standard Brands, www.americanstandard-us.com, (800) 442-1902

Page 107 left: Photo by Nomad_Soul / www.Shutterstock.com

Page 107 middle: www.Shutterstock.com

Page 107 right: Photo by Photobank.ch / www.Shutterstock.com

Page 108: Photo by Rodho / www.Shutterstock.com

Page 109 top: Photo by Baloncici / www.Shutterstock.com

Page 109 bottom: Photo by David Hughes / www.Shutterstock.com

Page 110 all: Photo courtesy of Madelli, Inc., www.madeli.com, (800) 819-6988

Page 111 top: Photo courtesy of Native Trails, Inc., www.nativetrails.net, (800) 786-0862

Page 111 bottom: Photo by Trubach / www.Shutterstock.com

Page 112: Photo courtesy of Native Trails, Inc., www.nativetrails.net, (800) 786-0862

Page 113 top: Photo by Eve Wheeler Photography / www.Shutterstock.com

Page 113 bottom: Photo courtesy of Native Trails, Inc., www.nativetrails.net, (800) 786-0862

Page 114: Photo courtesy of Native Trails, Inc., www.nativetrails.net, (800) 786-0862

Page 115 top: www.Shutterstock / www.Shutterstock.com

Page 115 bottom: Photo courtesy of Native Trails, Inc., www.nativetrails.net, (800) 786-0862

Page 116 top left: Photo courtesy of Grohe, www.groheamerica.com, (630) 582-7711

Page 116 top right: Photo courtesy of Native Trails, Inc., www.nativetrails.net, (800) 786-0862

Page 116 bottom: Photo courtesy of Lacava, www.lacava.com, (888) 522-2823

Page 117: Photo by albinutza / www.Shutterstock.com

Page 118 top: Photo by Kuznetsov Alexey / www.Shutterstock.com

Page 118 bottom: Photo by Tomasz Markowski / www.Shutterstock.com

Page 119 top: Photo by Rodho / www.Shutterstock.com

Page 119 bottom: Photo by Yampi / www.Shutterstock.com

Page 120 top: Photo courtesy of Jacuzzi, www.jacuzzi.com, (909) 606-1416

Page 120 bottom: Photo by Jorge Salcedo / www.Shutterstock.com

Page 121: Photo courtesy of Native Trails, Inc., www.nativetrails.net, (800) 786-0862

Page 122: Photo by Francesco Grossi; design by Paolo Demarco, courtesy of Lacava, www.lacava.com, (888) 522-2823

Page 123 top left: Photo by Jocic / www.Shutterstock.com

Page 123 top right: Photo by Yuyangc / www.Shutterstock.com

Page 123 bottom: Photo by Terekhov Igor / www.Shutterstock.com

Page 124 top: Photo courtesy of Lenova, www.lenovasinks.com, (877) 733-1098

Page 124 bottom: Photo courtesy of Native Trails, Inc., www.nativetrails.net, (800) 786-0862

Page 125 top: Photo courtesy of Ceramic Tiles of Italy, www.italiatiles.com

Page 125 bottom: Photo courtesy of Native Trails, Inc., www.nativetrails.net, (800) 786-0862

Page 126 bottom left: Photo courtesy of Madelli, Inc., www.madeli.com, (800) 819-6988

Page 126 bottom right: Photo courtesy of Pyrolave USA, www.pyrolave.com

Page 127: Photo courtesy of Native Trails, Inc., www.nativetrails.net, , (800) 786-0862

Page 128 top: Photo by Baloncici / www.Shutterstock.com

Page 128 bottom left: Photo courtesy of Champlain Stone, Ltd., www.champlainstone.com, (518) 623-2902

Page 128 bottom right: Photo courtesy of Kohler, www.kohlerco.com, (800) 4 KOHLER

Page 129 top left: Creative Publishing international

Page 129 top right: Photo courtesy of Xylem Group, LLC, www.xylem.biz, (866) 395-8112

Page 129 bottom: Photo courtesy of Kohler, www.kohlerco.com, (800) 4 KOHLER

Page 130: Rehan Qureshi / www.Shutterstock.com

Page 131: Photo courtesy of Hansgrohe, www.hansgrohe-usa.com, (800) 334-0455

Page 132 top left: Photo courtesy of Moen, www.moen.com, (800) 289-6636

Page 132 top right: Photo courtesy of Kohler, www.kohlerco.com, (800) 4 KOHLER

Page 132 bottom: Photo courtesy of Grohe, www.groheamerica.com, (630) 582-7711

Page 133 top left: Photo courtesy of Kohler, www.kohlerco.com, (800) 4 KOHLER

Page 133 top right: Photo courtesy of Hansgrohe, www.hansgrohe-usa.com, (800) 334-0455

Page 133 bottom: Photo courtesy of Native Trails, Inc., www.nativetrails.net, (800) 786-0862

Page 134 top left: Photo courtesy of Grohe, www.groheamerica.com, (630) 582-7711

Page 134 bottom left: Photo by Robert Perron, Istock/www.istock.com

Page 134 right: Photo courtesy of Grohe, www.groheamerica.com, (630) 582-7711

Page 135: Photo courtesy of Native Trails, Inc., www.nativetrails.net, (800) 786-0862

Page 136: Photo courtesy of American Standard Brands, www.americanstandard-us.com, (800) 442-1902

Page 137 top left: Photo courtesy of Grohe, www.groheamerica.com, (630) 582-7711

Page 137 bottom left: Photo courtesy of Grohe, www.groheamerica.com, (630) 582-7711

Page 137 right: Photo courtesy of Kohler, www.kohlerco.com, (800) 4 KOHLER

Page 138 left: Photo courtesy of Hakatai Enterprises, www.hakatai.com, (888) 667-2429

Page 138 bottom right: Photo courtesy of Brizo, www.brizo.com

Page 139 top: Creative Publishing international

Page 139 bottom: Photo by Baloncici / www.Shutterstock.com

Page 140 top left: Photo courtesy of Grohe, www.groheamerica.com, (630) 582-7711

Page 140 top right: Photo courtesy of Native Trails, Inc., www.nativetrails.net, (800) 786-0862

Page 140 bottom: Photo by Ivica Drusany / www.Shutterstock.com

Page 141 top left: Photo courtesy of Ceramic Tiles of Italy, www.italiatiles.com

Page 141 bottom left: Photo courtesy of Jacuzzi, www.jacuzzi.com, (909) 606-1416

Page 141 right: Photo courtesy of Kohler, www.kohlerco.com, (800) 4 KOHLER

Page 142: Photo by Jessie Walker

Page 143 top left: Photo courtesy of Crossville, Inc., www.crossvilleinc.com, (931) 484-2110

Page 143 top right: Photo by Ventura / www.Shutterstock.com

Page 143 bottom: Photo by Ioana Davies (Drutu) / www.Shutterstock.com

Page 144: Photo by Corinne Labastrous / www.Shutterstock.com

Page 145 top: Photo by Tr1sha / www.Shutterstock.com

Page 145 bottom: Photo by Roseburn3DStudio / www.Shutterstock.com

Page 146: Photo courtesy of Hakatai Enterprises, www.hakatai.com, (888) 667-2429

Page 147: Photo courtesy of Crossville, Inc., www.crossvilleinc.com, (931) 484-2110

Page 148 top left: Photo courtesy of Broan-NuTone, www.broan.com, (800) 558-1711

Page 148 top right: Photo courtesy of Broan-NuTone, www.broan.com, (800) 558-1711

Page 148 bottom: Creative Publishing international

Page 149: Photo by Tomasz Markowski / www.Shutterstock.com

Page 151 top: Photo courtesy of Moen, www.moen.com, (800) 289-6636

Page 151 bottom: Photo courtesy of Jacuzzi, www.jacuzzi.com, (909) 606-1416

Page 152 top: Photo courtesy of Harrell Remodeling, Inc/ www.harrell-remodeling.com

Page 152 bottom: Photo courtesy of Moen, www.moen.com, (800) 289-6636

Page 153: Photo courtesy of Moen, www.moen.com, (800) 289-6636

Page 154 top: Photo courtesy of Merillat® Cabinetry, www.merillat.com

Page 154 bottom: Photo courtesy of Merillat® Cabinetry, www.merillat.com

Page 155 top: Photo courtesy of Diamond Cabinets/www.diamond2.com

Page 155 bottom: Photo by Pics721 / www.Shutterstock.com

Page 156 top: Photo by aaphotograph / www.Shutterstock.com

Page 156 bottom: Photo courtesy of Finnleo Sauna and Steam/Saunatec, Inc.

Page 157 top: Photo courtesy of Ideal Standard International/ www.idealstandard.com

Page 157 bottom: photosphobos / www.Shutterstock.com

Page 158: Photo courtesy of VELUX America Inc., www.veluxusa.com, (800) 888-3589

Page 159 top left: Photo by Istock / www.istock.com

Page 159 top right: Photo courtesy of Solatube International, Inc., www.solatube.com, (888) 765-2882

Page 159 bottom left: Photo courtesy of Solatube International, Inc., www.solatube.com, (888) 765-2882

Page 159 bottom right: Photo courtesy of Solatube International, Inc., www.solatube.com, (888) 765-2882

Page 160: Photo courtesy of VELUX America Inc., www.veluxusa.com, (800) 888-3589

Page 161 top: Photo by Pics721 / www.Shutterstock.com

Page 161 bottom: Photo courtesy of VELUX America Inc., www.veluxusa.com, (800) 888-3589

Page 162: Photo courtesy of Hakatai Enterprises, www.hakatai.com, (888) 667-2429

Page 163 bottom left: Photo courtesy of Pittsburgh Corning Corporation, www.pittsburghcorning.com (800) 732-2499

Page 163 bottom right: Photo by Linda Oyama Bryan

Page 164 top: Creative Publishing international

Page 164 bottom: Photo courtesy of Jacuzzi, www.jacuzzi.com, (909) 606-1416

Page 165 top: Photo by David Hughes / www.Shutterstock.com

Page 165 bottom: Photo by Rade Kovac / www.Shutterstock.com

Page 166 top left: Creative Publishing international

Page 166 bottom left: Photo by Eric Roth

Page 166 right: Photo by Tor Lindqvist, Istock, www.istock.com

Page 167: Photo courtesy of Native Trails, Inc., www.nativetrails.net, (800) 786-0862

Page 168: Photo by Krzysztof, Istock, www.istock.com

Page 169 top: Photo courtesy of Moen, www.moen.com, (800) 289-6636

Page 169 bottom: Photo courtesy of Stone & Pewter Accents, www.stonepewteraccents.com, (310) 257-1300

Page 170 top: Photo courtesy of Moen, www.moen.com, (800) 289-6636

Page 170 bottom: Photo courtesy of Native Trails, Inc., www.nativetrails.net, (800) 786-0862

Page 171: Photo courtesy of Hansgrohe, www.hansgrohe-usa.com, (800) 334-0455

Page 172: Photo courtesy of Atlas Homewares, www.atlashomewares.com, (800) 799-6755

Page 173 top: Photo courtesy of Moen, www.moen.com, (800) 289-6636

Page 173 bottom: Photo courtesy of Atlas Homewares, www.atlashomewares.com, (800) 799-6755

Page 174: Photo courtesy of Hansgrohe, www.hansgrohe-usa.com, (800) 334-0455